Dr Patric. ....logist and head of adult mental health psychology services for NHS Lothian. She has worked for many years in the treatment of severe Anorexia Nervosa and is trained not only in cognitive behavioural therapy (CBT) but also in interpersonal psychotherapy (IPT), eye movement, desensitisation and reprocessing (EMDR) and cognitive behavioural system of psychotherapy (CBASP).

Professor Chris Freeman was an honorary professor at Queen Margaret University, Edinburgh. As consultant psychiatrist, he created and led services for eating disorders for over forty years, and ran outpatient, day-patient and inpatient units, and, most recently, an intensive home-treatment team for severe Anorexia Nervosa – all in the Edinburgh/South-East Scotland area.

The aim of the **Overcoming** series is to enable people with a range of common problems and disorders to take control of their own recovery programme.

Each title, with its specially tailored programme, is devised by a practising clinician using the latest techniques of cognitive behavioural therapy – techniques which have been shown to be highly effective in changing the way patients think about themselves and their problems.

Many books in the Overcoming series are recommended under the Reading Well scheme.

Titles in the series include:

OVERCOMING ANOREXIA NERVOSA

2nd Edition

A self-help guide using cognitive behavioural techniques

OVERCOMING

DR PATRICIA GRAHAM
and
PROFESSOR CHRISTOPHER FREEMAN

ROBINSON

ROBINSON

First published in Great Britain in 2019 by Robinson

A CIP catalogue record for this book
is available from the British Library.

IMPORTANT NOTE

This book is not intended as a substitute for medical advice or treatment.
Any person with a condition requiring medical attention should consult a
qualified medical practitioner or suitable therapist.

ISBN: 978-1-47214-131-6

Typeset in Bembo by Initial Typesetting Services, Edinburgh
Printed and bound in Great Britain by CPI Mackays

Papers used by Robinson are from well-managed forests and
other responsible sources.

Robinson
An imprint of
Little, Brown Book Group
Carmelite House
50 Victoria Embankment
London EC4Y 0DZ

An Hachette UK Company
www.hachette.co.uk
www.littlebrown.co.uk

Chris and I would like to dedicate this book to
Linda Irvine Fitzpatrick, for her truly inspirational
strategic vision, and without whom many of our services
just would not exist. Linda's genuine determination to
hear the voices of those who use and have used our
services has never wavered and has profoundly shaped
the quality of care in the NHS in Scotland.

Contents

Acknowledgements

I was asked by Professor Chris Freeman if I would like to update his *Overcoming Anorexia Nervosa* book. We discussed what we thought should change and agreed that the *content* should not change significantly but that we did need to bring it into the modern era – one that is dominated by technology. We also wanted to ensure that the information contained in the book is as up to date, relevant and applicable as possible. Both Chris and I really wanted to include the views and opinions of those people who have suffered from Anorexia Nervosa to help shape the new version of the book. We are hugely grateful to the eating disorder collective advocacy group of staff and volunteers at CAPS Independent Advocacy in Edinburgh, Niamh Allen, Amelia Austin, Casey Bevens, Freya Sewell and Sara Preston, all of whom helped reshape each chapter, especially the self-help sections.

We are especially grateful to Holly Wilson, trainee clinical psychologist, who provided updated references and exercised excellent formatting skills! The Lothian adult eating disorders specialist dieticians provided current dietetic advice, which has brought our guidance into line with current practice.

This book was revised in the last few months of Chris's life. He asked me if I wanted just *my* name on the front cover, but that would never have been my wish. This is Chris's book – I have merely given it a bit of a shine and polish. Chris was my mentor and my dear friend and, as for many, many others who loved him dearly, this world will never be quite the same without him. He was the wisest man I have ever known.

Patricia Graham

PART ONE

A GUIDE TO ANOREXIA NERVOSA

Introduction:
How to use this book

Awareness of the significance of eating disorders, and in particular Anorexia Nervosa, has greatly increased over the past few years. More and more people are aware that this is a very real, and very distressing condition, and one that should be treated, not dismissed.

This book is intended as a self-help guide for those who suffer from Anorexia Nervosa, or who fear that they may be developing a disturbing obsession with body weight and food. Part One sets out what is currently known about the disorder. In particular, it details the physical and psychological effects of the illness in the long term, from the effects of starvation on your well-being and future health, to the emotional factors that come into play when the disorder takes a grip. This is not intended to alarm or distress, but simply to make you aware of the seriousness of the condition, to persuade you of the benefits of healing yourself and to offer some reassurance that you are not alone in your fears about weight gain and food intake. Part Two sets out a sequence of steps through which you can begin to tackle the problem. This is above all a practical plan, and is offered as a flexible framework, not a rigid set of rules. No two people with Anorexia Nervosa are entirely alike, so you may well find that some of the psychological techniques do not suit you, and you may wish to adapt some elements of the treatment plan. The important point to remember is that the approach described here has proved a useful one for many.

In many cases of Anorexia Nervosa – particularly those where the illness is quite advanced – professional help will be necessary. How to go about finding the help you need, and what kinds of treatment are available, are questions dealt with in Chapter 6 of Part One. However, self-help techniques can be useful even to those simultaneously undergoing professional treatment, and in such circumstances this book may serve as a back-up.

The book may also serve as a useful tool when trying to explain to those around you just what is happening to you, and what you are trying to achieve. Anorexia Nervosa is a complex disorder. It is both very public and very private. Much of the behaviour is secret and causes the person with Anorexia Nervosa a great deal of guilt and distress. It is also a very public statement of distress: the starvation state is obvious to all those around, even if apparently denied by the sufferer. Anorexia Nervosa has been described as an addictive disorder – the addiction being not to food but to food deprivation, to starvation. In many ways it is similar to addiction to drugs or alcohol in terms of the cravings, the preoccupation with the addictive substance and the withdrawal symptoms when it is removed. However, there is one major difference: the alcoholic or drug addict can conquer the problem by avoiding drink or drugs completely; the person with Anorexia Nervosa cannot avoid food but has to learn to live with it and to develop a healthy, relaxed relationship with it. This is not easy: very few drug addicts or alcoholics can reach such a state of controlled, relaxed use after a prolonged period of addiction.

This, then, is the task that faces you, your friends and your family. We hope that this book will help you through that journey. As you read on, please bear in mind the following points:

- We have deliberately not used the term 'anorexic' to describe those with the disorder. The alternative 'person with anorexia' may seem unwieldy, but it is important to realise that you are not defined by the disorder; Anorexia Nervosa is a problem that can be overcome, not your whole identity. Try to think of yourself not as 'an anorexic', but as 'a person with Anorexia Nervosa'.

- Recovering from Anorexia Nervosa is not simple: there is no quick fix, no single solution. It will take time and hard work. Spend plenty of time preparing yourself for change. There is no need to rush things. Building up your motivation and strength to begin to change may be the most important step you take.

1

What is Anorexia Nervosa?

Anorexia Nervosa is an eating disorder, especially common in – but by no means confined to – women. The disorder usually begins in adolescence or early adulthood, the mean age of onset being fifteen years, but can start at any point between six and well into old age. If it does occur later in life it is more likely to be associated with severe psychological or physical disease (see Chapter 4). The central physical feature of Anorexia Nervosa is a very low body weight in the context of age, sex, development and physical health.

There are many physical and psychological symptoms secondary to starvation, but Anorexia Nervosa is principally a psychological disorder. Its characteristic feature is an intense fear of fatness and fear of loss of control regarding eating and body weight. An intense pursuit of thinness accompanies the fears. There is also nearly always a distortion of body image in which individuals perceive themselves as fat or overweight, even when everyone else thinks they are grossly underweight. There can often be a persistent lack of recognition of the seriousness of the low body weight, even when others point it out. Other methods, apart from starvation, may be employed to maintain low weight, such as exercising, vomiting or purging.

Although clinical studies have shown Anorexia Nervosa to be more prevalent in higher social classes, population studies show equal distribution in all social groups, which suggests that there is a degree of under-diagnosis and under-treatment of socially disadvantaged people with eating disorders. In some cases, what begins as a diet escalates. Success brings with it feelings of achievement and control. Often, individuals vulnerable to Anorexia Nervosa are in circumstances where they feel trapped and under pressure to succeed; or feel out of control in their lives. The rewards of exerting control over food intake and consequent weight loss become of exaggerated importance and may begin to dominate. Chapter 5 sets out some of the factors that make particular individuals vulnerable to developing Anorexia Nervosa.

Anorexia Nervosa is one of a group of eating disorders described in *Diagnostic and Statistical Manual of Mental Disorders* (5th edition, American Psychiatric Association) that is particularly prevalent in adolescent girls. Also in this group are Bulimia Nervosa, Binge Eating Disorder and a new eating and feeding disorder: Avoidant/Restrictive Food Intake Disorder. Bulimia Nervosa is characterised by episodes of binge eating, over a discrete period, often experienced with a sense of lack of control over eating. Binges may be very large, involving many thousands of calories, and are followed by purging, either with self-induced vomiting or laxative misuse, or a combination of both. People with Bulimia Nervosa are usually within the normal weight range. Individuals with Binge Eating Disorder have episodes similar to those with Bulimia Nervosa, but they do not purge. They may have periods of marked starvation between their binges. People with this disorder are generally in the normal or obese weight range. Those with Avoidant/ Restrictive Food Intake Disorder have an apparent lack of interest in eating, or food, in combination with a significant weight loss, nutritional deficiency or a dependency on oral supplements or enteral feeding. These eating disorders may exist independently and exclusively, but a person may experience different variants at different times.

Approximately 0.5 per cent of the female population experience Anorexia Nervosa, 2 per cent experience Bulimia Nervosa and a further 2 per cent experience Binge Eating Disorder. Prevalence estimates for the newly defined ARFID are not known yet. It has been estimated that male eating disorders account for 25 per cent of the Anorexia/ Bulimia Nervosa cases and 36 per cent of BED cases. The sex ratio for Anorexia Nervosa is approximately 10:1 female: male. If we include those in the early stages of the disorder or those who are partially recovered, these figures can be doubled; that is, some version of these disorders affects approximately 10 per cent of girls and women. (No corresponding figure for Bulimia Nervosa has yet been established.)

Anorexia Nervosa also carries a substantial risk of fatal outcome: follow-up studies of individuals severely affected by Anorexia Nervosa who were hospitalised, show that 0.5 to 1 per cent of these individuals will die of causes related to the disorder: 80 per cent from the physical effects of starvation and 20 per cent from suicide. A recent systematic review of thirty-six studies showed that the mortality ratio for all eating disorders is approximately three times that of the general population, and almost six times higher for Anorexia Nervosa. Anorexia Nervosa has the highest mortality rate of all mental disorders. These figures may be disturbing, even frightening; but it is important to remember that:

- Eating disorders are common: you are not alone. On the contrary, many others share your problem.
- In order to prepare yourself for treatment, it is good to learn as much as you can about Anorexia Nervosa and how it can be treated.

Some common myths about Anorexia Nervosa

Misguided, distorted and just plain wrong ideas about Anorexia Nervosa abound. Some of the most common are worth examining and refuting at the outset, because only with an accurate picture of the disorder can it be effectively tackled.

Myth: Anorexia Nervosa only occurs in women, particularly young women.	**Reality**: It occurs in men of all ages and in women of all ages.
Myth: Anorexia Nervosa is a disorder of privilege, occurring mainly in the upper and middle social classes.	**Reality:** People who attend a clinic tend to be from higher social classes, but it occurs across all social backgrounds and all levels of affluence.
Myth: Pressure or influence by the media causes Anorexia Nervosa.	**Reality:** This is too simple an explanation. Anorexia Nervosa has multiple causes. Anorexia Nervosa is not simply trying to be thin to be more attractive.
Myth: Anorexia Nervosa is caused by families, by certain patterns of family interaction and by mothers in particular.	**Reality:** This view, which is widely held, causes parents and daughters alike a great deal of distress and guilt. Most of the problems in families where a member has Anorexia Nervosa are a result of the disorder rather than the cause of it.
Myth: Anorexia Nervosa is not a serious disorder.	**Reality:** It clearly is. In many cases it is very difficult to treat. The physical complications are severe and the death rate among the most seriously affected is high.

Myth: Once you have Anorexia Nervosa you will never recover – you will always be 'an anorexic'.	**Reality:** This is not true. Follow-up studies show that recovery is possible even after as much as twelve years of continuous severe symptoms, and in our clinical experience, people can go on to recover fully after many years of suffering from Anorexia Nervosa.
Myth: Anorexia Nervosa is caused by simple dieting that gets out of control. Only a minority of people experience Anorexia Nervosa.	**Reality:** On its own, dieting does not cause Anorexia Nervosa. Many people have dieted at some time, and many have done so frequently.

How to distinguish between Anorexia Nervosa and dieting

Anorexia Nervosa is not caused by dieting. However, Anorexia Nervosa and dieting clearly do have certain things in common:

- Weight loss is the goal.
- To achieve weight loss, food intake is reduced.
- Exercise may be combined with a reduced food intake to increase, or speed up, weight loss.
- Calorie values are learned and computed, sometimes quite obsessively, to the extent that the person with Anorexia Nervosa can remember the calorific values

of all the foodstuffs they eat regularly without consulting a calorie guide.

However, despite these surface similarities, the differences are many and substantial. Someone on a diet, as opposed to someone with Anorexia Nervosa, will generally, although not exclusively:

- Admit to being a dieter, and often be keen to discuss the diet, target weight, feelings of deprivation, lapses and triumphs.
- Admit to feelings of deprivation and to having cravings for specific foods.
- Feel a sense of satisfaction from achieving an ideal weight, and be content to reach that level and not lose any more weight.
- Experience an increased interest in food, but try to steer clear of situations involving food so as to avoid temptation.
- Not be competitive with family members, friends or colleagues in terms of reduced food intake, i.e. not feel defeated if she finds that she has eaten more than another member of the family.
- Put their diet 'on hold' for special occasions that involve eating, such as a birthday meal or a Christmas dinner.
- Whether frequently or rarely, bend the rules of the regime, and not be unduly disturbed in so doing.
- Not be very consistent: weight loss from dieting is

usually uneven, with a dieter losing one pound one week and three the next, or even regaining lost weight through excessive rule-bending.

- Often fail: most diets are given up quickly and lost weight is regained.
- Work to a schedule: diets are generally time-specific, especially fad diets that promise a certain weight loss within a certain time-frame; e.g. 'Thin Thighs In Ten Days', or regimes embarked upon with a particular end-date in mind, such as the departure date for a foreign holiday.
- Have a reasonable goal – at least in terms of projected weight loss, if not always in terms of projected time taken to achieve it: thus, some diets seem spectacularly effective at the time, but much of the lost weight will be fluid, not fat, and therefore be quickly replaced.
- Eat rapidly in an attempt to satisfy hunger.
- Avoid people who are eating indulgently, or even normally, as this enhances their feelings of deprivation.
- Seek the support of others in their attempt to lose weight.

By contrast, the person experiencing Anorexia Nervosa will generally:

- Often deny being on a weight-loss diet.
- Not admit to feelings of deprivation, or to craving specific foods, particularly of the high-calorie variety.

- Tend to deny weight loss, and even attempt to hide it by wearing baggy, figure-concealing clothes.
- Not seem to become distressed by the close proximity of food, but rather actually to enjoy it: many people with Anorexia Nervosa develop a great interest in cookery and preparing food for other people.
- Spend long periods of time searching the internet and reading online recipes, looking at other people's food photos and foodie blogs.
- Tend to dish out unreasonably large helpings to other people at mealtimes; this may relate to the desire to eat less than others.
- Be wholly dominated by the desire to be thin, with an associated morbid fear of becoming fat.
- Continually revise target weight downwards.
- Tend to become obsessed with food– like the dieter – but rather than trying to avoid things associated with food, they will seek them out, for instance by studying cookery books, visiting supermarkets and cooking.
- Linger over food, chewing slowly and thoroughly.
- Tend to become increasingly phobic about eating in public, and may hoard food in order to eat alone and unobserved.
- See a distorted image, feeling fatter while getting thinner, and become increasingly sensitive and plagued by feelings of low self-worth.
- Link self-esteem inextricably with perceived control over body size and weight.

- Never break the rules – or actively fear doing so, and become deeply distressed if that happens, whereas a dieter may treat herself to the odd indulgence and at worst be annoyed afterwards.
- Tend to become very competitive and obsessive about achieving exactness during mealtimes and concerning calorie content of foods. Eating rituals may be mirrored by increasing obsessiveness in other areas of life, such as schoolwork and relationships.
- Tend to be rigid about what foods are and are not allowed, and find it difficult when meal plans change at the last minute.

How common is Anorexia Nervosa?

The short answer is that it is very common, although in our clinical experience people who experience Anorexia Nervosa can and do recover. The peak incidence of onset of Anorexia Nervosa is now fourteen to eighteen years old. The peak incidence rate for Bulimia Nervosa is fourteen to twenty-two years old. Binge Eating Disorder is mostly seen when someone is in their late teenage years or early twenties.

Reflections from Chapter 1

- What have I learned?

_____

_____

_____

_____

_____

_____

_____

- How can I put what I have learned into practice?

_____

_____

_____

_____

_____

_____

_____

- What can I do differently as a result of reading this chapter?

_____

_____

_____

_____

_____

_____

_____

2

How Anorexia Nervosa affects people physically and mentally

This chapter sets out to examine, in some detail, the physical and psychological effects of Anorexia Nervosa, including serious and potentially fatal complications. This is not intended to cause alarm. Indeed, frightening people has proved a rather ineffective way of inducing behavioural change. However, it is important that you know as much as possible about what is happening to you, so that you can make an informed decision if and when you decide that you want to instigate change.

Physical effects

There have been people with Anorexia Nervosa who have made a clear and informed decision that, for them, being thin is more important than halting the physical damage, such as osteoporosis (bone thinning), kidney damage and risks to the heart. On the other hand, there are many who, once they have seriously contemplated the harm and the likely long-term results, have made a clear and informed decision that they wish to change, even though that means gaining weight.

At this stage, try not to dwell on the issue of weight gain, which is the greatest mental stumbling block to anyone with Anorexia Nervosa. For now, try to look only at the effects that the disorder is having on your body. Reading this information may even help to begin the process of thinking about your body in a different way.

Symptoms of Anorexia Nervosa

The symptoms detailed in this book are the more common symptoms of Anorexia Nervosa. As with any chronic disorder, the longer Anorexia Nervosa persists, the more complications occur. There is also an increased risk as time goes on of major psychological disorders, such as depression, anxiety disorders and alcohol dependence, which can make treatment more difficult.

The metabolism

The human body is a masterpiece of engineering. When it is attacked by a disease organism, it creates antibodies to destroy the invader. When it is injured, it sends signals to the brain to indicate where it needs treatment. When it is starved of nutrition, it seeks to conserve what reserves of energy it has in order to protect vital tissue. This is why, as you continue to under-nourish your body, the speed at which you lose weight will lessen. Basically, your body is adapting to '*famine conditions*', seeking ways to burn calories at a slower rate and so to preserve your health. As your metabolic rate slows, so does your growth rate. In pre-pubescent individuals with Anorexia Nervosa, puberty is delayed; in women of menstruating age, periods may stop. The state of starvation causes feelings of fatigue and weakness as your body seeks to make you reduce physical activity and therefore conserve energy. In many cases, however, the psychological urge to increase activity and thus speed up weight loss will over-ride these physical feelings. As you seek to lose more and more weight, your body is actually pitching against you: hence that feeling, common to those with Anorexia Nervosa, that you are at war with your body.

Table: Common physical symptoms of Anorexia Nervosa

Symptoms	Fatigue
	Weakness
	Feeling cold
	Dizziness
	Chest pain
	Heart palpitations
	Constipation
	Diarrhoea
	Amenorrhea (lack of periods)
	Swollen ankles
	Puffy hands

If also vomiting …	Dental erosion
	Sore throat
	Hoarse voice
	Heartburn
Appearance	Dry hair
	Dry skin
	Pale skin
	Hair loss
	Lanugo (fine hair)
	Cracked lips
	Orange palms/yellow skin
	Green tinge to skin and swollen face
Silent symptoms	Osteoporosis (thinning of bones)
	Muscle wastage
	Brain shrinkage
	Impaired kidney functioning
	Immune system changes
	Ovary and uterus shrinkage
	Impaired fertility
	Anaemia
	Weakening of heart muscle
	Low white blood cells (to fight infection)

Ultimately, if starvation continues, the regulatory mechanisms of the body will be over-ridden. Epileptic fits are not uncommon in people with Anorexia Nervosa, usually occurring in the context of a disrupted internal environment.

Some people who have been exposed to long-term starvation, whether voluntarily or by force, find it very difficult to learn to eat again, and remain chronically underweight. There are examples of political hunger strikers who, even after they have called a halt to their deliberate fast, have found it very difficult to resume normal eating habits and have developed a syndrome very like Anorexia Nervosa. Some former prisoners of war or survivors of concentration camps have never managed to regain the weight they lost and have remained chronically thin. Such people often report that they cannot tolerate many kinds of food, or that they eat very slowly, and feel a marked bloating even after normal-sized meals. On the other hand, there are those who gain huge amounts of weight and feel a compulsion to eat as fast as possible and leave nothing on their plate.

Why do I have back pain?

Effects of mineral deficiency

The starved body will gradually become deficient in important minerals. This is due in the first place to a basic lack of nutrition but is greatly exacerbated by vomiting. Lack of minerals can have very serious consequences for your long-term as well as short-term health. Lack of calcium, for instance, the symptoms of which include weak muscles and back pain, can lead to the development of osteoporosis. Young people with Anorexia Nervosa can be as seriously at risk from this disease as women in their seventies. A lack of magnesium, indicated again by weak muscles, can lead to tetany (muscle tremors), while a lack of potassium, indicated by feelings of thirst and fatigue, can ultimately lead to heart problems. And while excess salt (sodium) can aggravate high blood pressure and fluid retention, a deficiency can cause severe dehydration and dangerously low blood pressure. Those with normal eating patterns will take in sufficient sodium as part of their daily diet without recourse to the salt cellar, but as the person with Anorexia Nervosa has reduced food intake greatly, salt intake will likewise be significantly lower.

Why is my skin dry?

The skin

The skin may become dry and crusted due to starvation and low levels of oestrogen and thyroid hormone. Fine downy hair, like the hair on babies, may grow all over the body. At first this has a 'peach fuzz' appearance, like the skin of an unripe peach, but the fine white hair can become quite long. This is called lanugo and is related to low oestrogen levels.

The skin may develop an orange tinge, particularly on the palms of hands and soles of feet, and on the rougher skin around knees, elbows and knuckles. This is caused by high levels of carotene in the blood (*carotenaemia*). Though it can be due to eating lots and lots of carrots, it is usually because the liver enzyme that breaks down carotene has failed due to starvation.

Why is it difficult to climb stairs?

Muscle wasting and muscle weakness (myopathy)

When you reduce your food intake severely, your body turns first to its reserves of fat to nourish itself. There comes a point when there is little or no fat left to lose, and then your body exists on what little food it takes in and by metabolising muscle. In extreme cases this includes heart muscle.

This muscle wastage results in a drawn and haggard appearance, like that of a much older person whose muscles are wasting, as a result of old age. The less muscle you have, the more slowly you will burn calories. Also, as the muscles are not getting all the nutrients they need, they often work even less well than would be predicted just from the wasting. Signs of severe myopathy are difficulty in climbing stairs or in standing up unaided from a squatting position, and a clumsy, flat-footed way of walking.

Why is my back sore?

Low back pain

Low back pain in Anorexia Nervosa is common; this is not usually due to osteoporosis or bone thinning. It is often caused because the spinal column doesn't have enough muscle support, posture becomes bad and this puts strain on the spinal joints. Osteoporosis is a silent condition and doesn't usually cause any symptoms until the fracture occurs. With marked starvation, the discs between the vertebrae and the spine become shrunken and less elastic and this can happen to ligaments around other joints. Pain on exercise is therefore common because the joints are less protected and less supported.

The brain

In advanced stages of starvation, shrinkage of the brain may occur. To try to keep the brain functioning properly, the body will utilise amino-acids usually reserved to form essential body proteins, further weakening other tissues.

Why do I feel dizzy and have chest pain?

The heart

In cases of severe starvation, the heart weakens and its ability to pump blood around the body is greatly reduced. Blood pressure lowers, which results in symptoms such as feelings of dizziness and faintness. In extreme cases, cardiomyopathy can develop: this is a condition characterised by the failure of the heart muscle to function efficiently, and can result in chest pains and palpitations.

The kidneys

Low blood pressure, resulting from starvation, also has an adverse effect on the kidneys, making it more difficult for them to function efficiently. They can become damaged by persistent dehydration and also when there are chronically low levels of potassium in the blood (potassium is lost rapidly when someone uses vomiting or laxatives to control weight).

Why do I feel full even if I have very little food?

Gastro-intestinal system changes

The whole of the gastro–intestinal system, from the throat to the rectum, eventually shrinks if the body is continually starved. This results in feelings of fullness even after very small amounts of food and drink have been consumed. Starvation also disrupts the activity of enzymes, active throughout the gut in the process of food digestion, and in bacteria growing more rapidly in the small bowel, leading to poor absorption of even the small amounts of food that are being eaten. Constipation is another common problem for those with Anorexia Nervosa and can cause severe abdominal pain as well as general dis–comfort. It is often in dealing with secondary problems, such as this, that professional help is first sought, and it is frequently from this point that Anorexia Nervosa is acknowledged.

Why does a wound take longer to heal than usual?

The immune system

The immune system is responsible for defending the body

against attack by bacteria, viruses and other agents of infection. In starving people, this immunity is very much impaired. The ability of the white blood cells to deal with invasive bacteria is reduced, the healing of wounds is grossly impaired (a problem exacerbated by a lack of calcium, which regulates blood clotting) and infection with unusual organisms, such as fungi, is much more common.

Why do I always feel cold?

Temperature regulation

When the metabolic rate is reduced, the result can be increased sensitivity to cold temperatures. Hypothermia is common among people with Anorexia Nervosa, partly due to hormonal changes, partly due to the loss of the essential body fat that we require to insulate us from the cold, and partly due to a resetting of the body's thermostat, which involves a part of the brain called the hypothalamus. Someone with Anorexia Nervosa will frequently feel cold and tired, and possibly experience spells of dizziness.

Why have my periods stopped?

The reproductive system

Starvation can impair fertility by causing the uterus and ovaries to shrink. Amenorrhea (cessation of menstruation) is an inevitable consequence. If a starving woman does become pregnant there is an increased risk of miscarriage, which is often the body's way of indicating that it cannot sustain a second life. If the foetus survives, there is a risk that the baby will be under-sized, under-nourished and subsequently liable to impairment in learning capacity in later life.

Why do I feel like I have so little energy?

Energy levels

For many people, the initial response to starvation is over-activity. Slowing down to the point of lethargy tends to occur only with severe malnutrition. For others, however, a lack of energy is experienced after even a small amount of weight loss. This variability is believed to reflect bio-logical adaptations to crises. For instance, a high level of energy is greatly desirable when searching for food in times of famine, while under-activity, induced by a sapping of energy, is useful for preserving essential body tissue. Thus, some people with Anorexia Nervosa develop a high activity level quite naturally, while for others it is a question of mentally over-riding the body's signals to preserve energy.

Why is my throat always sore?

Physical effects of vomiting

Repeated vomiting eventually causes dental damage, caused by stomach acids passing through the mouth frequently, gradually eroding the teeth. Another effect is a constant sore throat, which may be prone to bleeding. Heartburn is also common, as a result of gastric juices, produced by the stomach in response to eating, having no food to digest (because it has been vomited) and attacking the stomach walls. In the long term, this superfluity of gastric acid can lead to the development of stomach ulcers. Stomach juices contain a lot of potassium, so it can also result in potassium deficiency.

Why do I feel so bloated?

Physical effects of laxative abuse

Laxative abuse, another way of purging the body of food before it can be properly digested, strips the body of fluid, causing severe dehydration. It can also cause 'lazy bowel syndrome' – a condition where the bowel has become reliant on laxatives to function, and so comes to a halt when laxatives are not administered. This can result in water retention, bloating and chronic constipation.

Are the physical changes permanent?

The good news is that nearly all the physical complications of Anorexia Nervosa are reversible. Even the marked physical damage caused by very severe Anorexia Nervosa can be reversed – but only by weight gain and maintenance of a normal weight. In 1996, a long-term follow-up study of nearly two hundred women with an eating disorder was completed. In the cases of those who had resumed normal dietary habits and were considered 'cured', fertility levels and bone health had returned to normal. However, this was a slow process, in some cases taking up to five to ten years after complete recovery from severe Anorexia Nervosa. The rate of healing is much slower than the rate at which damage occurs – for example, the bone loss which occurs over two to three years of Anorexia Nervosa may take eight to ten years to reverse – and there may in some cases be enduring effects.

Women who have had no periods for many years may return to normal fertility. However, young girls who have primary amenorrhea – that is, whose periods never start – may permanently damage their reproductive capacity and not start to menstruate even if they gain normal weight in their twenties. Some small studies have shown marked brain shrinkage in severely ill individuals with Anorexia Nervosa; while this is to a great extent reversed if normal weight is regained, there is a suggestion that a degree of shrinkage may be permanent in some cases. Most people with Anorexia Nervosa, especially those who also have bulimia, will require extensive work to repair the damage done to their teeth.

Overall, however, the body has remarkable powers of recovery; the important point to remember is that it is never too late to get better.

Behavioural effects: changes in the way people act

Changes in activity

Many people with Anorexia Nervosa become highly active. They try to be constantly busy and on the move, and are often very reluctant to switch off and relax. They may exercise for long periods of time, or find excuses to indulge in calorie-burning activities, such as volunteering to fetch things, and therefore having to walk about or climb stairs, or setting out early to walk to a destination, rather than accepting a lift. Sitting still or doing nothing becomes increasingly alien to the person with Anorexia Nervosa, whose thoughts are focused on the issue of weight loss and body shape.

In some cases, a person with Anorexia Nervosa may become compulsive about exercise, using it as a weapon against weight gain. After eating, and especially if the intake is perceived as excessive, compulsive exercisers work out strenuously until a certain number of calories consumed have been burnt off. If for some reason exercise cannot happen, for instance if there is no privacy, there may be a tendency to become nervous and agitated, even going so far as to visualise the calories converting into fat; this can be an extremely tormenting experience for the individual.

When free to exercise, the person who is experiencing Anorexia Nervosa may do as much as time and strength will allow, which may increase, as Anorexia Nervosa takes its grip, to the extent that physical activity dominates the day, and becomes an all-consuming compulsion. As a result, many people with Anorexia Nervosa have very strict and exhausting daily routines.

Other weight-loss behaviours

Other behavioural patterns associated with Anorexia Nervosa, geared towards weight loss and/or against weight gain, include purging, by vomiting or using laxatives or diuretics after eating, in order to rid the body of food. This is the behaviour characteristic, as we have already seen, of Bulimia Nervosa.

People with Bulimia Nervosa are more likely to have been slightly overweight before embarking on a weight-loss diet and tend to eat much more normally than those with Anorexia Nervosa alone. However, their diet can be extremely volatile, ranging from a normal weight-loss programme to excessive over-eating followed by the urge to get rid of the food eaten, usually by self-induced vomiting.

As the latter is done with the utmost secrecy, people with Bulimia Nervosa are not easily identifiable, especially as their body weight will gravitate towards the norm.

Consequences of weight-loss behaviours

Behaviour geared towards weight loss such as starving, self-induced vomiting, laxative and diuretic misuse, and excessive exercising may have profound psychological, physiological and biochemical repercussions.

- Psychological repercussions include violent mood swings, feelings of isolation and depression, and the steady erosion of self-esteem.
- Physiological repercussions include dilation of the small intestine, which can cause feelings of extreme bloating and further aggravate existing constipation.
- Biochemical repercussions include dehydration and an imbalance in the body's electrolyte levels. Dehydration, caused by the lowered levels of blood potassium and chloride resulting from starvation, can cause extreme lethargy and physical weakness, tingling sensations in hands and feet, and, if very severe, heart irregularities.

The psychological effects of starvation: changes in thinking

Anorexia Nervosa is a disorder characterised by disturbed thinking. People with Anorexia Nervosa see the world very differently from other people, and their sense of self is dependent upon the narrowest of factors, namely, an ability to exercise control over food intake, and their consequent weight and shape. Thinking is further disturbed when the individual reaches the point of starvation, which induces a marked alteration in consciousness. Therefore, a person with Anorexia Nervosa who reaches the point of starvation must first gain weight before underlying psychological problems can be tackled.

In general terms, starvation will make thinking a slower process and short-term memory will be greatly impaired. In very marked starvation, the person with Anorexia Nervosa develops a slow, ponderous and rather slurred manner of speech, which makes it look as though there is great difficulty in thinking and speaking at the same time. The changes are believed to be caused by starvation affecting the frontal lobes of the brain. These exert an executive function over the rest of the brain, and provide the fine-tuning to personality, controlling such processes as judgement, making choices and giving emotional expression.

The inevitable consequences of the starvation state include poor concentration, indecisiveness, anxiety, emotional instability, social withdrawal and lack of libido (though many people with Anorexia Nervosa may avoid sexual relations because they have such a low opinion of their personal attractiveness). Each of these develops slowly, but over time they will become noticeable and effect a definite alteration in personality.

The marked changes in thinking, caused by severe starvation, can be categorised as follows:

Preoccupation with food

The most striking change in someone with Anorexia Nervosa is, of course, the person's preoccupation with food, which becomes involuntary and dominates not just conscious thought, but feelings and dreams. Ruminations regarding food that has already been consumed and food that is to be consumed prevail. Recipes may be collected and many people with Anorexia Nervosa develop a love of shopping for food, cooking and preparing food for others (their own is prepared and eaten separately). The internet, as a resource for recipes and blogs, may be used for hours on end. This over-riding preoccupation with food reduces the person's scope of thought and experience enormously.

A person with Anorexia Nervosa may become an extraordinarily picky eater and develop extremist food fads that exasperate those around them. Vegetarianism is especially common, and may take a particularly strict form, with an insistence on vegetarian cheese and gelatine-free products. This not only adds extra complications to the whole business of eating, it also rules out many foods and therefore equips the person with extra reasons to refuse to eat. A vegan diet offers even more food-refusal possibilities.

The action of eating tends, in itself, to become very ritualised. This is partly a ploy on the part of the person with Anorexia Nervosa to mask a reduced food intake, and partly a way to draw out the event. This ritualisation may include eating very slowly and chewing each mouthful a set number of times; eating items of food in a particular order; cutting food up into tiny pieces before commencing eating.

Social occasions that revolve around food may be dreaded by the person with Anorexia Nervosa, as spontaneous eating, governed by appetite, has become alien by the time the disorder has taken a serious hold. The person with Anorexia Nervosa is panic-stricken about the possibility of losing self-control, and thus over-eating, and also about the possibility of being pressurised by others to over-eat. Unfortunately for those with Anorexia Nervosa, food plays a huge role in our society and its celebrations. Occasions from birthdays to job promotions to holy festivals are all celebrated by eating larger quantities than normal. Food is one of the most common rewards we give our children when they are well behaved and is also often the means by which we comfort those in distress. As we are brought up this way, we become strongly inclined to use food as a treat or comfort, for ourselves and our friends and family, when we become adults. For most people this is not a problem, but for the person with Anorexia Nervosa, it can become a nightmare.

What may begin as merely the avoidance of food can eventually have dramatic and devastating effects on personal relationships. The person with Anorexia Nervosa may be able to cope for a certain length of time, but ultimately may find that the effort of resisting the temptations leads to hostility towards other people and avoidance of such events. Colleagues, family members or friends may feel hurt and bewildered by this behaviour, which may increase feelings of isolation and loneliness, allowing the disorder to develop an even greater dominance.

Rigidity

Starvation causes thinking to become very rigid and inflexible. This is what is commonly referred to as 'black-and-white thinking', where a person can distinguish only between extremes of right and wrong, good and bad, nice and horrible, and loses the ability to distinguish shades of meaning. This greatly hampers the capacity to think in abstract terms; the starving person can work only with very concrete ideas. Amenability to rational argument is also greatly reduced: the mind refuses to entertain ideas and concepts other than its own.

Immature thinking

In Anorexia Nervosa there is a reversion to an immature system of thinking which involves the person believing that they are immune to the principles that govern other people's lives. For example, if an adult tells a seven-year-old boy that, in ten years' time, he will be more than happy to kiss girls, he will both believe and not believe what the adult says. He will accept that seventeen-year-old boys like to kiss girls, probably because he has witnessed such things, but he will not accept that he will behave the same way when he is seventeen. Similarly, someone with Anorexia Nervosa may accept that, yes, Anorexia Nervosa is an illness that distorts the way a person sees themselves, but will not accept that it affects them in this way.

Obsessionality

Anorexia Nervosa brings an increase in obsessionality. This is not restricted to thoughts of and behaviour around food; it can affect many areas. A compulsion towards neatness and order, punctuality and cleanliness may develop. These obsessions can cause the individual's day to be packed with time-consuming rituals, from folding down the sheets of the bed in a certain way to showering before and after meals or exercise. They may even serve as a way of keeping activity levels high. However, in some cases, the person with Anorexia Nervosa may excuse themselves entirely from these rules and instead, impose them on other people – becoming intolerant, for example, of those who are late, or make a mess, or refuse to finish the food that is on their plate. In short, the person with Anorexia Nervosa has become unable to cope with those who do not cater to these obsessions, and this can increase the sense of isolation felt and the sense of frustration and helplessness felt by others.

Stereotyped thinking and behaviour

This refers to doing and saying the same things over and over again, such as constantly asking for reassurance and repeating phrases and rituals. This kind of thinking makes it almost impossible for the person with Anorexia Nervosa to progress from one thought or idea, and thus during an argument they will be unable to develop ideas or defences, as they would were they not starving. People often describe arguments with someone with Anorexia Nervosa as being like going around in ever-decreasing circles. As the illness takes hold, it seems to squeeze out the ability to think, so that the frame of reference and any development from it becomes smaller and smaller.

Reflections from Chapter 2

- What have I learned?

_____

_____

_____

_____

_____

_____

_____

- How can I put what I have learned into practice?

_____

_____

_____

_____

_____

_____

_____

- What can I do differently as a result of reading this chapter?

_____

_____

_____

_____

_____

_____

_____

3

Anorexia Nervosa and other disorders

Anorexia Nervosa and Bulimia Nervosa

The behaviour of someone with Anorexia Nervosa exists on a continuum between the two extremes of absolute abstinence and Bulimia Nervosa. (For more information on Bulimia Nervosa see Peter Cooper's book in this series, *Overcoming Bulimia Nervosa and Binge Eating*.) The eating patterns of the person with a restricting type of Anorexia Nervosa involve severely restricting food intake, and closely monitoring and pursuing thinness. Typically, all foods considered fattening, such as carbohydrates and fats, are banned, and bulky, low-calorie foods, such as vegetables and fruit, are allowed.

If the individual exists in a state of starvation for a sufficient length of time, the rigid diet may be broken by a desperate eating binge in which everything and anything available is eaten rapidly. In such an episode, food may be eaten straight from tins, insufficiently defrosted from the freezer – whatever is to hand, without thought as to its calorie content or appetising nature. The food is usually eaten extremely quickly, without being enjoyed and frequently without being properly chewed and digested. This kind of episode is called a binge-eating or bulimic episode, as it is followed by feelings of self-loathing and disgust, which prompt the person to get rid of the food as quickly as possible. This may be done by self-induced vomiting or by taking a large quantity of laxatives, in order to get rid of the food before the calories have been absorbed. In our clinical experience, approximately 40–50 per cent of people with Anorexia Nervosa experience binge-eating or bulimic episodes.

A type of Anorexia Nervosa called binge eating/purging is a different story from 'pure', restricting Anorexia Nervosa, and is characterised by feelings of guilt, self-disgust and failure. It may also be self-punishing, in that the person may regard the post-binge purging as a form of self-punishment. In contrast to the control and perfectionism of Anorexia Nervosa, Bulimia Nervosa tends to be associated with impulsivity, and can include or lead to such behaviours as alcohol or drug abuse, sexual promiscuity or stealing. The feelings of self-disgust experienced by the person with Bulimia Nervosa may reach the extremes of self-harm, such as body-cutting or burning, and may prompt suicide attempts. The behaviour of the person with Bulimia Nervosa, often characterised by high impulsivity, emotional instability, explosive relationships and self-destructive tendencies, is similar to the condition of Borderline Personality Disorder.

The concept of addiction is also closely related to the behaviour of the person with Bulimia Nervosa, as the binges are compulsive and secretive, and the individual comes to rely on them as a form of comfort, or escape hatch, when they find themselves unable to deal with life's problems.

I had to have a 'perfect' day, in terms of eating, or it would end with a binge. Some days I knew in the morning that I would go home and do it, and I would stop in at the supermarket on the way home to stock up. Everything would be ready-to-eat, and I would buy things that normally I would never allow myself, things like pies, chocolate and always ice-cream. I always made sure I had a two-litre bottle of lemonade as well, as it made the process of being sick much easier afterwards. While I was eating I felt kind of high, but as I began to feel full to bursting point, the panic would set in. As soon as the binge was finished, I would go to the bathroom and begin to make myself sick. This involved putting my fingers down my throat, and sometimes taking gulps of water from the tap to help the food come up. When I was done, I felt quite light-headed and sort of cleansed.

Lucy

The two forms of Anorexia Nervosa, restricting and binge/purge, are not mutually exclusive. As mentioned, the person who restricts will occasionally have bouts of bingeing and the person with Bulimia Nervosa will have episodes of self-starvation. However, if the picture is more of bingeing and purging, body weight will be closer to normal.

Whatever the primary behaviour type, at the core of Anorexia Nervosa is the individual's fear of gaining weight, and the efforts to avoid this.

Anorexia Nervosa and other psychological disorders

Although the 'classical' picture of Anorexia Nervosa is now widely recognised, the disorder often merges into and overlaps with many other psychological conditions. Approximately 60 per cent of people who have Anorexia Nervosa will suffer from a second psychological disorder.

Anorexia Nervosa and depression

When using the term 'depression' here, we are not just referring to everyday sadness and unhappiness. The characteristics that go to make up what psychiatrists and psychologists would call a depressive illness or major depressive disorder include persistent low mood or lack of feelings; sleep disturbance; lack of energy; poor memory; poor concentration; feelings of guilt and worthlessness; and a very negative or pessimistic view of yourself, your past and the world around you. Sufferers say they feel empty or dead inside; it is as though their feelings were paralysed. Many cultures have a quite different set of words to describe this feeling – in the nineteenth century we used the word 'melancholia' – but unfortunately in contemporary Western society we use the word 'depression' to cover a wide range of feelings from mild, brief unhappiness to persistent and all-embracing despair.

Low mood, persistent depression and depressive illness often coexist with Anorexia Nervosa. The relationship is a complex one. Some people quite rapidly get 'dieting depression' when they go on a strict diet – indeed, their mood may drop even before any significant weight loss has occurred. Others get the opposite reaction and may experience a marked sense of elation, increased energy and well-being when they first embark on a diet. At some stage almost all people who are in a state of severe starvation will get depressed. Sometimes this is a gradual process, the depression getting deeper and deeper the more marked the weight loss; sometimes it can be quite sudden. I have one patient who seems to be fine until her weight drops below 40 kg (88 lb). At 42 kg (93 lb) she can be cheerful, bubbly and full of energy, but at 39 kg (86 lb) she is physically and mentally slowed up, has a very pessimistic view of herself and the world around her, and experiences major symptoms of depression. This depression does not respond to antidepressant drugs or to psychotherapy but is dispelled by a small amount of weight gain.

In other individuals the weight loss can be extremely severe before depression sets in. Very occasionally, individuals who have starved themselves close to the point of death (23–4 kg or 50–3 lb) still appear quite cheerful. However, in these individuals the apparently happy mood is often very brittle and may hide a great deal of personal pain and distress. In these cases, there seems to be a clear relationship between low mood and the starvation state.

In some individuals it appears that the depression may have come first. Many women whose Anorexia Nervosa began in adolescence can in retrospect identify a clear period of depression over a few weeks or months before they started dieting. It was almost as though their dieting was a response to their low mood, and sometimes a partial solution to it. When they came for treatment there was no sign of the depression at all; but when they recovered from their Anorexia Nervosa either they were able to remember and recognise the depressive period they'd had, or, more distressingly, their depression came back when they gave up their individual coping mechanisms.

A third pattern is when depression occurs after many years of symptoms of Anorexia Nervosa. Depression is a common occurrence in many chronic and disabling disorders, and it is difficult to establish whether there is anything special or different about the depression that occurs in chronic Anorexia Nervosa compared with that which may occur in someone with a chronic physical condition such as rheumatoid arthritis, epilepsy or diabetes. The depression may be a result of having to cope with a serious disabling disorder that affects all aspects of life.

In a fourth situation, Anorexia Nervosa and depression occur simultaneously. This is particularly distressing because the individual is beset at the same time by two equally disabling and painful conditions. One positive aspect, however, is that people in this group do tend to seek help early.

Anorexia Nervosa and obsessional disorders

An obsession is a repeated, intrusive thought that comes into your mind against your will, and that is difficult or impossible to resist. Usually there is a need to do or think something to neutralise or counteract the thought. Compulsions are the rituals that people carry out in response to their obsessional thoughts. Examples are counting, touching, washing and checking rituals. Obsessional thoughts may revolve around themes such as fear of contamination, fear of being harmed or harming others, the need for order or symmetry, or the need to feel clean or to feel things are 'just right'. These thoughts are not hallucinations. Obsessional individuals do not hear voices; they know the thoughts they have are their own, even though they feel alienated from them and do their best to resist them.

Anorexia Nervosa and Obsessive–Compulsive Disorder overlap in two areas. First, many of the core symptoms of Anorexia Nervosa have a definite obsessional quality to them. The repeated thoughts about food, fatness, body shape and size fit all the criteria for obsessional symptoms.

The case of Richard is an example.

Richard was a nineteen-year-old student with a three-year history of Anorexia Nervosa. His diet had become extremely restricted so that he could only eat white food off large white plates. The plates had to be scrupulously clean and he had to wash them several times before they could be used; no one else could touch the plate. His main diet consisted of boiled white fish. He would boil the fish in plain unsalted water and stand over the pan with a paper towel, dabbing the globules of oil and fat which rose to the surface. The fish would be boiled until it was mush; then it would be 'safe' to eat. Although much of his behaviour was about avoiding calories, eating mainly protein and particularly avoiding fat, there was a definite 'magical', ritualistic quality to it. The whiteness clearly symbolised purity and cleanliness and was seen as good. He was not particularly afraid of germs; it was just that the food had to feel and look right before he could eat it. Richard's obsessionality got worse the thinner he got, and largely disappeared when he recovered from his Anorexia Nervosa.

Second, about half of all individuals with Anorexia Nervosa develop obsessional thoughts in areas not directly related to food. They have quite separate checking, counting or touching rituals or a repeated need for order, symmetry or having things feel 'just right'. The case of Jane is an example.

Jane is a thirty-two-year-old woman who has clear symptoms of both Anorexia Nervosa and Obsessive-Compulsive Disorder. Many of her obsessions, but not all of them, revolve around food. She takes three hours to prepare her evening meal, even though she ends up eating virtually the same every night. She has to weigh and check things repeatedly, and the meal has to feel and look just right before she can eat it. She is constantly on the move; while she is preparing food, she goes backwards and forwards between the kitchen and the living room, deliberately only taking one thing at a time. When she moves round the kitchen she always takes the longest distance between two points. These are ways of keeping moving and burning off calories. She lives in a second-floor flat and has to climb up and down the stairs at least ten times each evening before she can feel satisfied. She will always find a rational reason for this but knows that she is quite driven. She eventually sits down exhausted about 9 p.m. in front of the TV to eat her meal and allows herself an hour of relaxation.

Jane's other obsessions include cleanliness and tidiness. She cleans the house every day when she gets home from work and tidies it up, even though she lives alone and the room has remained untouched since she left it that morning. Some of these activities obviously also involve exercise, but others are to do with order and symmetry: these include having all the book spines on the book shelf even, the magazines neatly arranged, the ornaments on the mantelpiece positioned in an exactly symmetrical way and the pictures all checked to see that they are straight.

Jane's hands are red, raw and scaly from repeated washing, and the cuticles around her fingernails are all inflamed.

Jane has no time for any social or recreational activities; work, food preparation, exercising and cleaning take up nineteen hours a day. She gets approximately five hours' sleep.

For a person to be diagnosed with Obsessive-Compulsive Disorder requires more than simply being obsessed or pre-occupied. People may be obsessed with books or model railways or animal welfare and spend a great deal of time thinking about their subject; however, in most cases there is no sense of resistance, the activities are often pleasurable or give a sense of satisfaction, and there is no sense that by carrying out some sort of ritual you will magically alter what has been done.

Anorexia Nervosa and anxiety disorders

Anxiety is a very common symptom in individuals with Anorexia Nervosa and has multiple triggers. There is anxiety about food, eating, body shape, the need to exercise and feelings of being out of control.

More specific anxiety symptoms can be seen in a number of areas:

- *Social anxiety about eating.* Many people with Anorexia Nervosa find eating in company very stressful, preferring to eat alone, and disliking being observed while eating. This can escalate into a severe social phobia where eating in public seems to be absolutely impossible.

- *Social anxiety about appearance.* This too can become severe, leading to very withdrawn and isolating behaviour. Beset by feelings of disgust with appearance, convinced about being fat and repulsive, the individual does not want to be seen at all. Some people become virtually housebound, going out only early in the morning or late at night, covering their faces with long hair and wearing bulky, loose-fitting clothes to hide their appearance completely.

- *Agoraphobia.* In our experience this is not common in those who present with Anorexia Nervosa. Whereas social anxiety refers to a fear of being observed or scrutinised, agoraphobia is a fear of open spaces, of being far from home or of being trapped in a crowd. So, agoraphobia refers to a fear of the situation rather than fear of the individuals within it.
- *Anxiety leading to panic attacks*. In contrast, these are common. A panic attack is where anxiety escalates rapidly and one feels overwhelmed by feelings of anxiety, sweating, rapid heartbeat and dizziness. Often this is associated with rapid breathing (hyperventilation).

For more information on anxiety disorders and how to cope with them, see the books in this series by Helen Kennerley, *Overcoming Anxiety*, and Gillian Butler, *Overcoming Social Anxiety and Shyness*.

Reflections from Chapter 3

- What have I learned?

_____

_____

_____

_____

_____

_____

- How can I put what I have learned into practice?

_____

_____

_____

_____

_____

_____

_____

- What can I do differently as a result of reading this chapter?

_____

_____

_____

_____

_____

_____

_____

4

Anorexia Nervosa in other population groups

Anorexia Nervosa in children

As discussed in Chapter 1, Anorexia Nervosa usually begins in adolescence; however, it is now known that Anorexia Nervosa can be identified in children as young as six, and such childhood cases are being increasingly reported. Since diagnosis in children has been quite rare and controversial, care must be taken to rule out the presence of another primary causal condition. Perhaps in part as a result of such caution, diagnosis of Anorexia Nervosa in children is frequently delayed. This is highly unfortunate, for the condition can have devastating effects if undetected in pre-pubescent children, permanently damaging growth and development; early diagnosis and competent treatment are vital.

The incidence of childhood Anorexia Nervosa is still not known; however, it has become clear that, while the disorder is less common in children than in adolescents or adults, the numbers are rising. A common finding with childhood Anorexia Nervosa is the relatively high percentage of boys who have the disorder. In adults with Anorexia Nervosa, men account for approximately 11 per cent of cases, whereas in children, boys have been reported to account for between 20 and 25 per cent. It is not yet clear if this is a definite gender difference or whether younger boys are simply more likely to come to medical attention than girls of the same age. One interesting difference has emerged in that while girls tend to say they want to be thin for aesthetic reasons, boys often give reasons of health and fitness.

The main differences between children and adolescents for those with Anorexia Nervosa

Physical deterioration is more rapid in children, possibly because they have less fatty tissue in their bodies. However, this may appear to be a problem of growth or failure to reach puberty, rather than the more obvious weight loss characteristic of adolescent Anorexia Nervosa. Depressive symptoms appear earlier and more commonly in childhood Anorexia Nervosa, possibly as a result of the faster rate of deterioration, and anorexic symptoms escalate with weight loss, creating a vicious circle. While the core features (behavioural and psychological) of the condition are similar to those in adolescents and adults, bingeing and laxative abuse are less common among children.

It is possible that childhood Anorexia Nervosa may represent a more biological/genetic form of the disorder.

Prognosis in this group is comparatively poor. Only two-thirds make a full recovery, the remainder continuing to experience difficulties. Persistent amenorrhea occurs in about 30 per cent of this group, and long-term repercussions include delayed growth, infertility and osteoporosis.

Complications of Anorexia Nervosa in children

Physical complications include:

- **Growth impairment.** If the onset of the condition occurs before puberty, there can be permanent effects on adult stature. If the child is still ill at age fourteen, he or she is unlikely to be able to make good lost growth.
- **Exacerbated effects of starvation.** Children reach a more severe degree of emaciation for a similar degree of weight loss, as they have smaller fat reserves than adolescents or adults.
- **Dehydration.** Children are more susceptible than adults and deteriorate rapidly when vomiting, laxative abuse or fluid refusal or restriction occur.
- **Delayed sexual maturation.** Puberty may be delayed; in girls, periods never start, and permanent damage may be done to the potential for breast growth.
- **Osteoporosis (bone thinning).** This may be more severe since, as the disorder starts before the bones are fully mineralised, normal peak bone mass is not reached.

Psychological complications include:

- *Depressive symptoms.* These are very commonly reported.
- *Regressive behaviour.* When distressed, children often regress behaviourally, so 'tantrums' in children with Anorexia Nervosa should be viewed as an index of distress rather than naughtiness to be punished.
- *Lack of insight.* Children think more concretely than adults and are often deeply fearful. Thus, they often misunderstand 'treatment' as punishment for 'being bad'.
- *Low self-esteem and feelings of rejection.* Hospitalisation may exacerbate low self-image and feelings of parental rejection or punishment.

Social/familial complications affect:

- *Family functioning.* A severely ill child creates stress for the whole family. The ill child may have rigid rules which become inflexible, especially around mealtimes. What we do know, from clinical experience and research, is that certain behaviours in the family may unwittingly maintain the disorder, but there is no evidence to suggest that those behaviours have actually caused it.
- *Parents.* Parents may blame themselves for the disorder. Psychological problems in parents may make it harder for them to take charge of their child's eating.

- *Siblings.* Siblings suffer emotionally, often feeling deprived or guilty. They may be overfed by their sibling with Anorexia Nervosa and may become embarrassed to bring friends home.
- *Schooling.* If the child becomes ill enough to be kept away from school, the loss will not only be an academic loss but also on peer group socialisation. When the child does attend school, there may be experiences of being teased and rejection by peers. If these experiences are chronic, they may result in a deficient social network, poorly developed social skills or social phobic symptoms, thus exacerbating the child's sense of isolation and depression.

How to recognise if a child has Anorexia Nervosa

Weight loss or the failure to gain weight accompanied by food refusal may indicate a number of different conditions. The following checklist should be helpful.

- In Anorexia Nervosa, the core psychopathology, 'intense fear of gaining weight or of becoming fat', is prominent.
- There is a significant disturbance in the way body shape or weight is experienced by the young person and there is a 'persistent lack of recognition of the seriousness of the low body weight'.
- Food refusal, fads and fetishes are common problems in childhood, especially with young children. In

most instances it is not difficult to distinguish these from Anorexia Nervosa, since the characteristic pre-occupation with body weight and shape is absent.

- The term 'selective eating' applies to children who appear to exist on typically two or three different foods. These tend to be carbohydrate-based, such as biscuits, cereal, chips or particular kinds of sand-wiches. It is quite common and there is usually no weight loss or anorexic psychopathology.

- Bulimia Nervosa, characterised by out-of-control eating behaviour swinging between the extremes of food avoidance and over-eating usually followed by purging to protect against weight gain, is very rare in children, especially in those under fourteen.

- Appetite loss may be secondary to depression or anx-iety. Depressed individuals often suffer from a lack of appetite, so children with a history of not eating should be checked for other disorders such as Major Depressive Disorder.

- Appetite loss may be secondary to a medical disor-der, e.g. inflammatory bowel disease, malignancy or endocrine disorder. The core psychopathology of Anorexia Nervosa will be absent.

- Appetite loss may be secondary to some other cause, e.g. organic brain disease, psychosis, illicit drug abuse (Ecstasy, amphetamines) or prescribed drugs.

The child's school may be able to provide important in-formation about the child's eating habits and the academic, social and emotional competence. However, if the school is involved, remember that the staff may also have little experience of Anorexia Nervosa. Early recognition of Anorexia Nervosa is very important but is also frightening, especially for parents. Signs to look out for which may help you to identify that there is a problem include the following:

1. Avoidance of mealtimes.
2. Restriction of food.
3. Weight loss or failure to gain weight during the period of pre-adolescent growth (ten to fourteen years) in the absence of any physical or other mental illnesses.
4. Preoccupation with body weight and weighing several times a day.
5. Becoming anxious around about mealtimes.
6. Trying to hide weight loss.
7. Being preoccupied with energy intake (counting calories).
8. A distorted view of body shape and size.
9. An intense fear of fatness with an accompanied denial of hunger.

Early warning signs of Anorexia Nervosa in children

Many pre-pubescent children are now diet-conscious, often internalising their mothers' dieting and media messages. Anorexia Nervosa can start in the absence of overt dieting (for example, after an episode of viral illness causing loss of appetite), or as a diet with a friend. How can early Anorexia Nervosa be distinguished from 'normal' dieting?

- **Severity of the eating restraint.** Even early in Anorexia Nervosa, over-control of eating and an inability to break a diet will be evident. The child may become very distressed if pressed to eat what may have been a previously favourite food (e.g. ice-cream).

- **Denial and deception.** The child may deny experiencing hunger. He or she may lie about what has been eaten, and conceal or dispose of food (for example, flushing a school lunch down the toilet). Deceptive behaviour is not a feature of normal dieting but that of an addict to starvation.

- **Hyperactivity and compulsive exercising.** Relentless activity (running rather than walking, standing rather than sitting, staying awake rather than sleeping) are characteristic features of Anorexia Nervosa. The compulsive quality and solitary nature of this activity distinguishes it as pathological. Often exercising will be denied.

- **Rate and extent of weight loss.** Weight loss is rapid and the child may try to conceal it to avoid concern. Normal pre-pubescent children rarely lose weight on a diet, and if they do they will proudly demonstrate their achievement.

- **Behaviour around food.** A child with Anorexia Nervosa as young as age ten may insist on preparing her own food and even that of the whole family. The child may cook elaborate, high-calorie meals for others without eating themselves. Eating may become ritualistic, with food being cut into tiny pieces or eaten very slowly. Some children will insist on eating less than others and may confine eating to night time or in private. Some children may vomit after eating. Such actions on the whole are not those of a normal dieter, who will try to avoid the temptation of being around food.

- *Depressed mood.* The child is likely to show signs of social withdrawal and irritability. Sleep disturbance in childhood is an indicator of depression and Anorexia Nervosa, and is a cause for concern.

- *Obsessive-compulsive behaviour.* Obsessive preoccupation with diet and exercise, and with rituals concerning food or exercising, are typical of someone with Anorexia Nervosa. Other obsessions are less common but do occur.

Treatment of children with Anorexia Nervosa

Treatment of Anorexia Nervosa is always a lot more complex than simple weight restoration, and this is especially so for children, for whom the family system has a relatively important influence. For all children with Anorexia Nervosa (all those under eighteen years) the family will be involved in treatment. Formal family therapy is not necessarily the preferred choice; family counselling may do just as well. For those families that do not feel comfortable with family counselling or family therapy, parental counselling alongside individual psychotherapy for the child is just as effective and may be preferred. Whatever option is taken, it is important that the family receives support, guidance and education, since Anorexia Nervosa can have a devastating effect on family functioning.

Individual psychological therapy is a valuable adjunct to family or parental counselling in children with Anorexia Nervosa but is not a replacement for it. There is no consensus regarding which type of individual therapy should be used; it is possible that therapist empathy, continuity and a developmental approach may be more important than the type of therapy itself. Emotional change takes longer to bring about than weight change, so long-term therapy may be needed.

Physical treatments and drug treatment may also be used. No drugs directly affect the course of Anorexia Nervosa, but some may help with particular symptoms. If depression coexists, low doses of antidepressants, taken with food, may help. If the child suffers delayed gastric emptying, a drug may be prescribed to help this. (NB: Prolonged food restriction causes muscular atrophy of the entire digestive tract. This leads to slow stomach emptying also called 'delayed gastric emptying' and can be the cause of trapped gas, bloating and abdominal distention.)

Dietary treatment is obviously important, as a major goal in the treatment of children with Anorexia Nervosa is weight restoration. This is especially important in children on the brink of puberty, as growth potential is continually being lost. If the child has reached a very low weight, a skilled re-feeding programme should be implemented and the advice of a dietician be sought; in less extreme cases, a high-energy balanced diet using the portion system – a way to consider a meal plan without counting calories – is advisable (see page 181). Vitamin supplements are rarely necessary. Food supplements may be useful, especially in severe cases where food refusal is marked, and also if the child's weight is low but stable and the child is refusing further normal food. However, they should be used in addition to, not instead of, a normal mixed diet.

Hospitalisation is likely to be necessary if the child's weight has fallen to less than 70 per cent of the normal level for their age; if there are physical complications (e.g. dehydration, circulatory failure or persistent or bloody vomiting); or when there is depressed mood or other psychiatric disturbance in the child or parents.

Anorexia Nervosa in men

Anorexia Nervosa is considerably less prevalent in men than in women; men account for only about 11 per cent of cases. Apart from a few obvious sex-related differences in symptoms (e.g. amenorrhea occurs only in women), on the whole there appear to be few differences between the sexes in terms of the physical features of the disorder. Weight loss, emaciation, hormonal changes and starvation-related symptoms are found in both males and females. Men also display the characteristic fear of fatness, refusal to maintain normal weight and rigidity in thinking.

However, there are three major factors that do differentiate men and women with Anorexia Nervosa:

- Males diagnosed with Anorexia Nervosa are often obese to begin with, as opposed to females who 'feel' overweight but may not actually be overweight.
- Men with Anorexia Nervosa, more often than women, diet in order to attain goals in a particular sport, such as running, swimming or athletics.
- More men than women with Anorexia Nervosa began dieting to prevent themselves from developing medical conditions witnessed in other family members, such as coronary disease and diabetes.

On the whole, from our clinical experience, most men who develop Anorexia Nervosa are more obsessed than women with the exercise component. They are often compulsive exercisers, spending long hours each day jogging or doing press-ups and other exercises. While they are often as obsessed about their diet as women, they do not often show the same interest in cooking and recipes. While bingeing, vomiting and anxiety eating are as common in male Anorexia Nervosa as in female Anorexia Nervosa, there is often less laxative abuse.

Certain features common in men with Anorexia Nervosa include conscientiousness and obsessionality as children: these applied to approximately a third of one group studied, while a similar proportion described dietary problems, either obesity or finicky eating habits. The presence of significant life events also appears common in the year preceding the onset of the disorder. Identifiable triggers are often related to a change in circumstances, whether through the death or departure of a loved one or a move to a new city.

Men, just like women, are strongly influenced by cultural pressure regarding appearance and roles. Over the years the pressures and expectations imposed on men by society have changed. While the traditional emphasis on strength and power is still propagated through tough, fighting, hero types in films, contemporary trends also require high levels of career success with less regard for personal relationships. Yet it is also seen as important to have a partner. Thus, men are subject to conflicting demands: on the one hand to show power and strength, reflected in career and appearance, and on the other to acknowledge and express emotional needs, and as a result there may be a certain amount of internal conflict.

Anorexia Nervosa in the elderly

Contrary to popular thought, Anorexia Nervosa is not restricted to the young; it can start at any time in the life cycle, including during old age. Criteria for the diagnosis of late-onset Anorexia Nervosa are the same as those for adolescents: self-induced starvation and a morbid fear of fatness, along with denial of the seriousness of the low body weight. The pattern of this disorder varies greatly: in some it follows a lifelong preoccupation with weight and dieting, whereas in others there may have been no previous eating disorders.

Eating disorders are becoming more common in the elderly. Two reasons have been put forward to explain this increase. First, there has been a dramatic increase in the incidence of eating disorders in the last thirty years. Since at least 20 per cent of these disorders are chronic, and not all of those affected recover by the end of their reproductive life, some are likely to still have the disorder in their old age. Second, it is possible that even elderly women are beginning to succumb to the social pressures to be slim.

The diagnosis of Anorexia Nervosa in elderly patients may be more complex than in younger people, for a number of reasons. Elderly patients may be more reluctant to discuss psychological issues, eating habits or sexual issues. In some cases, weight loss may have been initiated by coexisting medical or psychiatric disorders but sustained by the individual thereafter. Weight loss may also be a symptom of one or more of the serious medical conditions that become more common during and after the forties, or be associated with major depressive symptoms, common in later years; in the latter case, there is no weight preoccupation or fear of fatness driving the weight loss. In any event, unexplained weight loss in an elderly person needs careful investigation and eating disorders should be considered among the possible causes.

As is common with eating disorders in younger individuals, many older people with Anorexia Nervosa also have other psychiatric problems, particularly anxiety, depression and perfectionism. Overly controlled personalities are often vulnerable, especially to remembered childhood neglect or emotional distress. It seems that childhood experiences of being teased or abused remain salient and sensitive issues for some and may manifest in an eating disorder when memories are exacerbated by a change in situation or circumstances, for example through the loss of a spouse or close friend.

There seems to be evidence that developmental milestones or phase-of-life events may serve as stressors for vulnerable women at any age, triggering Anorexia Nervosa as a maladaptive response. Younger patients report that rigorous dieting gives them an enhanced feeling of control when going through periods of loss and uncertainty. In later life, eating disorders may represent a reaction to continuing interpersonal loss – children leaving home, retirement from a job, or the death of friends or a spouse – and a similar perceived need to exercise control over some area of life.

It is important to view Anorexia Nervosa in its context. Its incidence among older women may be increasing as pressure mounts to retain physical attractiveness and sexuality. It has been suggested that some elderly women may become obsessed with thinness as a way of trying to avoid the ageing process. The picture of Anorexia Nervosa in the elderly closely resembles that seen in younger people. Indeed, the fear of ageing and loss of sexual power and attractiveness may be as traumatic for older women as the teenage fear of not attaining the necessary perceived standards, and may be dealt with by similar psychological mechanisms.

Reflections from Chapter 4

- What have I learned?

_____

_____

_____

_____

_____

_____

_____

- How can I put what I have learned into practice?

_____

_____

_____

_____

_____

_____

_____

• What can I do differently as a result of reading this chapter?

_____

_____

_____

_____

_____

_____

_____

5

What causes Anorexia Nervosa?

Anorexia Nervosa is rarely if ever caused by any one single factor – there are nearly always several factors involved – and each individual with Anorexia Nervosa is unique. This means that there are many possible contributing causes for the condition in any one person. This chapter sets out explanations generated by different schools of thought. You may find that one or more of these applies to you, or triggers thoughts of other factors that are unique to you.

It is useful to look at the causes of Anorexia Nervosa in three categories:

1. Factors that make you vulnerable to developing the disorder.
2. Factors that might trigger the disorder.
3. Factors that maintain the disorder, once you've got it.

A single factor may act in all three ways, but it is often the case that quite separate factors are involved in the three stages.

Stage I: Factors that make you vulnerable to Anorexia Nervosa

It is important to understand that Anorexia Nervosa can be caused by factors from within; these are the biological or psychological factors, from experience or from the family environment. Anorexia Nervosa cannot be accounted for by one over-arching theory, but only by an approach that considers life experiences in all areas.

While Anorexia Nervosa is distinct from other eating disorders such as Bulimia Nervosa or obesity, the themes across the three are similar: the use of food, shape and weight as a means of expressing and or controlling distress.

Early feeding difficulties

Many children develop early feeding difficulties, for a wide variety of reasons. It could be that the child is a naturally picky eater; or that the parent who is responsible for feeding has a strained relationship with food, or has a limited knowledge of how to feed a child appropriately.

There is now good evidence to indicate that psychiatric disorders in parents have the potential to interfere with their childrearing skills and the emotional development of their children. Eating disorders are an important type of psychiatric disorder prevalent in women of childbearing age. The effect of pregnancy on a woman's body may have a lot to do with this. After all, there are few conditions that cause such rapid and radical change in body weight and shape, and this can trigger a fear of fatness where it previously did not exist. Many young mothers experience a slump in self-esteem because of weight gain during pregnancy, and this can often be the beginning of years of dieting. Slimming magazines recount tale upon tale of women who struggled for years with their weight and who date the beginning of their weight gain back to their first pregnancy. Of course, concerns about body weight may have existed long before a pregnancy.

If a mother has an eating disorder it can affect her child in a number of ways. If she is preoccupied with her own body weight to the extent that she rarely considers her own needs when it comes to eating – that is, if she eats what and when she feels she 'should', rather than eating when she is hungry – this may reduce her sensitivity to her infant's needs. In short, she may have lost the ability to recognise natural feeding needs. Those who suffer from an eating disorder also frequently have difficulties in their interpersonal relationships, which can extend to the relationships they have with their children.

In adolescence, the child can become very vulnerable to cultural ideals. Supermodels such as Kate Moss and Jodie Kidd, who are extremely thin yet considered to be extremely attractive, may make a teenage girl, struggling to come to terms with budding breasts and the remains of baby fat, feel overweight and ungainly by comparison. A parent who is equally unhappy with his or her own 'non-ideal' body shape may reinforce the teenager's concerns. If the parent has very strong attitudes regarding shape, weight and diet, s/he may influence the child's attitude tremendously.

Comments suggesting that the child is too fat or too greedy may cause great distress. Problems can also arise if the child models his or her behaviour on a parent who has an eating disorder.

One of the difficulties in examining childhood eating patterns and attitudes to body weight is that this is mostly done in retrospect, when the individual has matured and already developed an eating disorder. From this perspective it is often tempting to look back and exaggerate any feeding abnormalities in childhood. Such methods of enquiry tend to lack rigour and fail to generate scientifically reliable data.

Genetic predisposition

There is a tendency for eating disorders, like other psychiatric disorders, to cluster in families. The children of parents with an eating disorder have been found to be much more at risk of developing a similar disorder than those whose parents had a healthy attitude towards food. While the findings are nowhere near specific enough to distinguish environmental causes (i.e. learned habits) from genetic (i.e. inherited) causes, there is more to suggest that the genetic explanation is the stronger one.

Studies have shown that there is a genetic predisposition to Anorexia Nervosa and other eating disorders. One study of twins showed that if one of a pair of monozygotic (identical) twins developed Anorexia Nervosa, then the other was four to five times more likely to develop the disorder than in the case of non-identical twins. This finding, along with the evidence that shows that first–degree relatives (children/parents/siblings) of patients with Anorexia Nervosa are at an increased risk of developing the condition compared to the general population, is firm evidence that there is a strong genetic predisposition towards development of this disorder.

Biological factors

As a species, we are very well adapted to starvation. Consider a situation such as a famine. For the famine-struck society to survive, there has to be at least a small group, particularly of women, who can cope with starvation to the extent that they survive for many months, even years, to ensure that children can be born and cared for.

There must also be a group of people whose energy levels are maintained, and who respond to starvation by becoming over-active. These are the individuals who can plan and perform essential tasks despite their weakened physical state: search for food, rebuild shelters, sow and harvest crops. It also makes sense, biologically speaking, to have a group of people who become inactive and die fairly quickly, thus reducing demand on dwindling food stocks.

Starvation has a radical effect on the chemical levels in the brain, particularly levels of serotonin, which stimulates hunger and craving for particular foodstuffs and is related to the development of obsessionality. Generally speaking, serotonin is released in the brain when we start eating. The surge of serotonin, which occurs particularly with a high-carbohydrate meal, is important in producing feelings of fullness and the desire to stop eating. On the other hand, very low levels of serotonin produce hunger and sometimes restlessness. It is interesting to note that serotonin levels drop before ovulation; this may go some way towards explaining why some women have increased food cravings at this time.

Other chemical messengers stimulated by starvation come from the stomach and intestines. An important one is cholecystokinin (CCK). Low levels of CCK produce feelings of hunger and craving.

Family structure

The stereotype of the 'anorexic' family is a negative one, in which the parents are overly protective and interfering and have very high expectations of their offspring. This is a somewhat misleading model, and many differences claimed to exist between the so-called 'normal' and the 'anorexic' family have been shown not to apply consistently. However, there are some features of family life that do seem to relate to the development of Anorexia Nervosa. These are:

- *A general avoidance of conflict within the family.* This may be due to an overbearing parent or to some unspoken fear that should conflicts be acknowledged, they will become uncontrollable. In such a family environment, individuals will often lose (or never develop) the ability to express and work through troublesome emotions, or to confront those of others, and become unnaturally afraid of conflict even outside the family. Such people may take a pacifying role in later life, making severe compromises themselves in order to avoid conflict with others.

- *One parent tending to be over-involved with a child, while the other parent is more passive.* For example, the mother may be solely concerned with the children while the father is absent or adopts a distant attitude.

- *Family rules and sense of identity so strong that it becomes difficult for any member to express individuality.* For instance, if a family has a long tradition of producing first-rate doctors, it can be difficult for a teenager to express the wish to work in the arts, as such a wish will be seen almost as a betrayal of the family.

- *Abuse, whether of a sexual, physical or emotional nature.* Sexual abuse may take the form of incestuous relationships between parents and children, or between siblings, or the toleration of sexual abuse by a family friend or relative of a child. Physical abuse may take the form of beatings, administered by a parent or older sibling, or neglect. Emotional abuse may take the form of verbal bullying and deliberate miscommunication.

- *High-achieving parents who have similar expectations of their children.* In many cases, the child has internalised these high expectations, or may have developed them naturally. This can result in a situation where a child feels afraid of failure and regards any effort it makes as worthless unless it is 100 per cent successful.

- *Acute sibling rivalry.* This may be created by parents and teachers who constantly compare siblings and make remarks such as, 'Your sister wouldn't do a thing like that.' However, this rivalry can also arise between siblings without any external forces coming to bear. For example, one sixteen-year-old girl felt very much in the shadow of her elder sister and remarked that 'everything she touched turned to gold', while she herself felt that she had had to work hard to achieve anything. Things came to a climax when she entered a race, for which she had diligently trained, and her sister, who had not, won it. The sixteen-year-old did not consider the fact that her sister was older and stronger, but took this event as proof that she was less able. In consequence she began a diet, in order to be fitter and run faster, but within a year she had developed Anorexia Nervosa.

Adolescent crisis

Adolescence is the peak time for the onset of Anorexia Nervosa. It is in the early teens that a person develops their sense of identity and their views on the world around them. This can be a period of great uncertainty in terms of academic ability, sexuality and social skills. Severe weight loss can halt or delay development in all three areas.

The period of transition between childhood and adulthood is a very tricky one. It is an age when the desire to be older and more mature becomes very powerful, as do the seductions of adulthood (as viewed from a young perspective) such as drinking, having sex and making money. This frantic desire to take on the mantle of adulthood can result in teenagers 'growing up too quickly', or behaving in ways for which they are, as yet, emotionally unsuited, such as embarking on sexual relationships at a point where they are still uncomfortable with the physical changes wrought by puberty. Alternatively, teenagers may find it enormously difficult to let childhood go, not just because they are apprehensive about the idea of being an adult, but also because those around them, particularly parents, may prefer them to remain childlike.

It is an important part of the growing-up process that young people can take 'risks', such as asking someone for a date and therefore risking rejection. It is also important that they are able to do this against the backdrop of a secure home environment, where there are no risks. This risk-taking is essential as it enables the individual to establish a degree of self-reliance, to develop confidence and engage with the world in a non-fearful way. If the individual is prevented from acting independently and self-sufficiently, most commonly by over-protective parenting, their progress may be even more difficult than it would be normally.

Of course, on the part of the vast majority of parents, such over-protective behaviour is not malicious interference. Usually they just want the best for their child and feel that this can only be achieved by exerting external control over their lives, perhaps in the form of pushing them academically and/or athletically. Often this is accompanied by the opinion that time spent with friends and boyfriends is wasted time, and so these activities are dismissed as trivial or actively disapproved of. Initially, a child will toe the line in order to avoid censure from or conflict with parents. However, if the child continues to behave this way, accepting parental dictates wholesale and doing the utmost to avoid conflict, feelings of pressure and entrapment can develop. The child's urge is to say 'no', to make their own demands, to rebel. If the child feels that they cannot articulate these feelings then they may, subconsciously, seek other ways of saying 'no'.

One of these ways is by refusing to eat. The put-upon adolescent comes to see the body weight as the only arena in their life over which any control may be exerted. Losing weight can provide an enormous feeling of relief, as it provides concrete proof of that control. It can also become a powerful statement of rejection directed at the family and home life. Losing weight can generate feelings of empowerment and superiority in an individual suffering from low self-esteem.

Social pressure to be slim for females

The Western ideal of feminine beauty has been a slender one since the 1920s. Back then, women smoked, took amphetamines and exercised in order to achieve the boyish figure that was currently in vogue. However, this mania for fashion-ability was pretty much restricted to the upper classes. Nowadays, every level of society is aware of fashion.

Magazines show us pictures of Victoria's Secret Models, while the internet details the strict diets with images of a glamorous world that does not tolerate imperfection, particularly the avoidable imperfection of fatness. Hollywood film companies are so determined to provide images of female perfection that they often employ body doubles for nude scenes; actresses routinely have bits of their bodies airbrushed out of the final cut if they are deemed too plump. A recent American survey provided the shocking finding that, so phobic has society become about fatness, men would rather date a heroin addict than an overweight woman.

Little wonder, then, that young people growing up in this environment become obsessive about their weight and feel that, above all other aspects of themselves, this is the key to attractiveness. Magazines may very well advise on the need for adequate vitamin intake and healthy attitudes, but they will invariably accompany this sensible advice with pictures of stick-thin models in their fashion spreads. Though this may seem trivial from an adult perspective, it is necessary to remember that for an adolescent, the issue of attractiveness is one of paramount importance. Therefore, the urge to be thin can outweigh all other aspirations.

For women there is an added complication. While film stars and celebrities have the legs of teenagers, they are also voluptuous. For most women, this combination is elusive. When they diet, their breasts reduce and they appear more boyish. Without recourse to surgery, they are caught between two ideals of beauty. This reflects many women's experience of life as well. They still feel caught between the need to be a successful, independent career woman and an attractive partner and loving, nurturing mother. This can be very confusing and distressing, and thus the pursuit of thinness, above everything else, can be something of a relief. Some women can convince themselves, with a helping hand from media-generated ideals, that being slim will solve all their problems, and iron out all contradictions.

The trouble is that the only problem thinness solves is the 'problem' of fatness. Being slender will not make any other area of life easier. It will not make you good at your job, popular or more loved. However, lack of 'results' in these other areas can often propel the person to pursue thinness all the more obsessively, long after they have achieved their original goal, as they have become so entrenched in the notion that thinness can solve everything. Many people who don't suffer from Anorexia Nervosa suffer from this belief, and throughout their lives devote time, effort and money to dieting and exercise regimes, which may serve only to undermine their confidence, by not delivering them from their perceived state of imperfection. However, for the person vulnerable to Anorexia Nervosa, this can be the point at which they become divorced from reality and see weight loss as the ultimate objective.

Search for autonomy

When we are children we are generally content to be seen as part of a family unit and to be identified as such. When we reach adolescence, however, the great pursuit of autonomy begins. This is a natural and essential rite of passage, and for most people it goes relatively smoothly. Of course, there will be family showdowns about clothes and haircuts, suitable friends and career ambitions, but most families are able to adjust to change and give burgeoning personalities enough breathing space to grow. It is when the family is unable to adjust that problems can arise.

For instance, a family that prides itself on producing lawyers may react badly against a teenager who has determined that she will go to veterinary college. They may withdraw financial and emotional support in order to bully the child into following the family tradition. The outcome can go either of two ways. The child may react by leaving the family unit and doing her own thing, or buckle under family pressure, do as they are told and develop a sense of resentment. In the latter case, where the young student feels that there is no control over the future and identity, there may be an attempt to establish autonomy in another way. Eating is one of the classic ways of doing this, as it is so central to family life. By refusing to eat, or developing peculiar or picky habits, the youngster is demonstrating autonomy in front of the family.

This desire for autonomy does not rear its head only in adolescence. It can arise if a sibling perceives that they are in the shadow of a more 'successful' brother or sister. The desire to be thin may arise from a need to establish an identity that is other than that of 'less successful sibling'. It can also arise if a woman finds herself submerged in the role of mother and wife and seeks to be seen as an individual rather than just an appendage of her husband and children.

However it happens, the pursuit of thinness is often based on a need to be seen as an individual, and to feel that self-will can be exercised, if only in one area of life. Thus, the beleaguered adolescent who refuses to finish lunch may be someone who is screaming to be allowed autonomy but can find no other outlet for it.

My father was determined that I went to his old university and studied the same subjects as he had, namely physics and maths. I didn't know how to say no to him. In fact, no one in my family knew how to do that. I did as I was told, even though I had wanted to study English literature and it was actually my best subject. The summer before I left home to begin university, we went on a family holiday to Belgium, and it was then that I began not eating. It became like a game, to see how much I could get away with not eating each mealtime. I don't remember feeling hungry or lethargic. I think the fact that I was the one in charge gave me a real buzz. When we got home and I found that I'd lost nearly three-quarters of a stone [9 lbs], I felt great. It was the first time I really felt like I was doing something that I wanted to do.

Karen

Low self-esteem

Low self-esteem can run in families. Parents with a low opinion of themselves may pass it on to their children by comparing them unfavourably to other people's offspring. This can result in children growing up with the belief that they are not as worthy as others and having little self-confidence. Low self-esteem can develop in adolescence, when young people invariably agonise over how they match up to others and become self-critical, or when crises, such as loss of occupation or desertion by a partner, occur. Low self-esteem can be dangerous: it makes people very vulnerable, prompting them to accept relationships that may be bullying and unhealthy, or poorly paid jobs where they are put upon by others who see their lack of confidence and exploit it. It can also lead to depression, to a recurrence of illnesses and to a severely reduced enjoyment of life.

When low self-esteem is recognised as the root of the problems, there are ways to deal with it. There are excellent self-help guides (for example, the book by Melanie Fennell in this series), courses and therapy sessions that can go a great way to changing individuals' perception of themselves. However, when low self-esteem is not identified as the problem, and the person continues to labour under the notion that they simply do not match up to others, the solutions sought can be unhealthy in the extreme. Alcoholism is one example. Many alcoholics turn to drink as a way of masking their negative feelings about themselves and, in a sense, escaping from themselves. Anorexia Nervosa is another. By unloading all those self-critical thoughts on to body image, a person can convince themselves that, if only a stone was lost or even two stones or three stones, life would be happier.

A sense of achievement is often accompanied with loss of weight, which will heighten self-esteem. If the weight loss continues after the target weight has been achieved, it may be that self-esteem is now so strongly identified with weight loss that to gain weight – even if it did not rise above the original target minimum – would be severely detrimental to it. Many people with Anorexia Nervosa know that, by starving themselves, they are not tackling the real problems of their lives but have become so dependent on extreme thinness as a way of bolstering their self-esteem that they cannot make the break from it. This is not to say that within their emaciated bodies they are bursting with confidence; quite the reverse, in fact. The problem is that, as they see it, to gain weight would make them feel even worse.

Sexual abuse

Studies of the histories of people with eating disorders have found a much higher rate of sexual abuse than among women with no psychological problem. However, the rate of such abuse was no higher than among women with other psychological disturbances, such as depression. Sexual abuse therefore seems to be associated with psychological disturbance in general, rather than with eating disorders in particular.

There has been much debate recently as to whether women who have experienced sexual abuse or been coerced into unwanted sexual experiences are more likely to develop difficulties associated with eating. So far, the results have been inconclusive. For some people, the link between sexual abuse and eating disorders is quite clear. Some sexual abuse victims feel that they have lost control of their lives, and that the eating disorder re-establishes some form of control, however negative. Some even choose to alter their body shape to the extent that they reduce their desirability and therefore stave off further sexual approaches. Others speak of guilt, disgust and self-hatred, and use the eating disorder as a form of self-punishment. An important feature common to those studied is that their lives had many other major problems and upheavals occurring simultaneously. Hence it is likely that the eating disorders were the result of cumulative problems rather than the single factor of abuse.

It has also been discovered that the eating disorder may have a functional purpose; that is, it is used in an attempt to solve a problem. For example, by developing an eating disorder, a person may be trying to punish the abusive parent, or the parent who failed to protect them adequately. In this instance, the changes in eating patterns and consequent eating disorder are a means of causing disruption and of attaining control. In short, the eating disorder is a stick with which to beat those who are felt to be to blame.

Certainly, for those who have suffered sexual abuse and are now experiencing eating difficulties, examining and working with their feelings relating to abuse can be helpful. A useful resource for those in this situation may be the book in this series on *Overcoming Childhood Trauma*.

Dealing with separation and loss

Few things in life have the devastating impact of permanent loss or separation. Losing a parent, a close friend, even a beloved family pet, can turn an individual's world upside down. Death is particularly hard, as most of us are without a mechanism to deal with it, especially if we have no religious faith to provide us with some form of comfort, and as those around us are suffering too. For a child it can be even worse, as a death throws up new questions of their own mortality and that of the people around them. Many children who lose one parent become morbidly obsessed with the idea that they will lose the other.

When we lose someone close to us, we experience enormous sorrow which can permeate our general consciousness for a time and lead to depression. A common feature of depression is loss of appetite, and so weight loss is fairly common in this situation. For most people, even children, this is a temporary state, and body weight will return to normal during the process of coming to terms with the loss. Even so, the journey of grief and mourning can be a long and hard one, requiring us to acknowledge our emotional needs and dependencies, and to recognise our own vulnerability. For some, the process of grieving seems an impossible task, perhaps because they feel that the pain will be too great if they give into it or perhaps because they believe that no one fully understands their feelings. They may use food as a means of numbing themselves to emotional pain. Starvation can cause this state of numbness and protect the individual by delaying the active process of grief and mourning. Because eating will restore normal feelings, they may choose to continue with the starvation.

Another way of deflecting pain is by bingeing food and then purging the body of it. Eating will provide a sense of comfort and the subsequent feelings of self-loathing and desire to purge the body will occupy the mind and stave off other feelings. In this sense, Bulimia Nervosa can be seen as a way of crowding out unwanted emotions.

In recent years increasing amounts of evidence have been gathered to support the clinical observation that children and adolescents exposed to undesirable events are at a significantly increased risk of developing depression and other forms of psychopathology, including eating disorders. The most difficult kind of events to deal with are those involving the loss of someone close. This degree of crisis can also trigger adults towards depression and, in some cases, Anorexia Nervosa.

There are many reasons why a person may be prompted to lose weight and subsequently develop Anorexia Nervosa. It may be that they are influenced by external pressure to be slim, or by a desire to assert their autonomy within a restrictive family structure. They may be reacting against sexual abuse or the loss of a loved one. Whatever the reasons, it is important to remember at this stage that not all diets result in Anorexia Nervosa and not all cases of Anorexia Nervosa derive from a desire to fit into size-six jeans.

Evidence suggests that self-esteem is one of the most critical factors in the development of the disorder. The life circumstances in which Anorexia Nervosa occurs are varied. They may be fraught and difficult, with the vulnerable individual feeling under pressure from parents, put upon by others, or restricted in future choices. Alternatively, these circumstances may be excellent, with supportive family, unconditional love and great prospects for the future. The common element is that the individual who develops Anorexia Nervosa, for whatever reason, experiences chronically low self-esteem.

Personality type is also an important factor. Where one personality type reacts to adolescent conflict by indulging in drug-taking or sexual activity, another personality type may exercise self-control, in the form of abstaining from food.

Finally, an inability to cope with change, be it in family structure, body shape or approaching adulthood, can make an individual very vulnerable to the development of Anorexia Nervosa, as can a similar inability in those around her.

The most important thing to be aware of is that no two cases of Anorexia Nervosa, or any other eating disorder, are exactly alike, and no one factor is at the root of the condition. It is also important to be aware of the fact that Anorexia Nervosa creates a state of mind that actually maintains the disease. We shall explore this point further in the final section of this chapter.

Stage II: Factors that trigger Anorexia Nervosa

The second stage in the development of Anorexia Nervosa consists of the period between the establishment in a vulnerable individual of a behavioural precursor, such as dieting, through to the establishment of Anorexia Nervosa in its own right. Some of the factors described above appear to put the individual more *at risk* for an eating disorder by increasing the likelihood they may diet. While dieting is the common stage-setter for the disorder of Anorexia Nervosa, there are still many people who diet, successfully or unsuccessfully, without suffering from Anorexia Nervosa; the critical issue is what factors combine with a diet to result in Anorexia Nervosa. One particularly prominent element in this process is low self-esteem. There is also evidence that particular kinds of adolescent conflict and difficulty, and particular personality types, tend to promote the disorder more than others.

Among the factors that have been considered to precipitate the development of the disorder are those normal to healthy adolescent development, including the onset of puberty, development of relationships (especially with the opposite sex) and leaving home, as well as more distressing events including loss of relatives, illness and others' negative comments about their appearance. Circumstances that are identified as stressful and capable of making growing up difficult are, predictably, parental psychiatric illness, parental conflict, parental loss, disturbance in older siblings and major family crises. Difficulties may arise when an individual is unable to adapt well to change, or when close family or friends are similarly unable to adapt themselves well to the individual's development and maturity. These failures to adapt are usually inextricably linked, one factor enhancing the effect of another.

Stage III: Factors that maintain Anorexia Nervosa

There are many factors that contribute to the maintenance of Anorexia Nervosa once it has become established. The behaviour of the person will have changed, and so will the behaviour of others close to them; therefore, they will now be used to being treated differently by others. Whether or not this change in behaviour of the person with Anorexia Nervosa involves adoption of the 'sick' role, the individual with Anorexia Nervosa will rarely seek help. Self-starvation and the physiological consequences of under-nutrition result in a vicious circle of emotional angst and behavioural disturbance. Both the concrete behavioural pattern and emotional upset must be interrupted and addressed if recovery is to be possible.

Adolescence, as noted above, is a period of transition; it is a time for trying new behaviour and gaining new experiences. Withdrawal at this time is common, be it via drug abuse, running away or phobic reactions, and Anorexia Nervosa may be considered to be such a withdrawal behaviour. Once energy and effort have been invested in establishing the disorder, the individual is not going to give it up without a fight. The Anorexia Nervosa will have become so much a part of their identity and their coping strategy for difficult aspects of their life that it will be difficult for them to envisage the benefits of not having it. Some of the following elements may contribute towards maintenance of the disorder and increase difficulties regarding breaking the pattern:

1. Core features of Anorexia Nervosa itself, including 'intense fear of becoming fat'.
2. The rewards of weight loss, including feelings of self-control and often approval from others before any severe loss is apparent; also avoidance of the difficult changes that occur in adolescence.
3. Body-image distortion, which increases with increasing weight loss.
4. Biological effects of weight loss, which due to the starvation syndrome help to maintain the disorder, including preoccupation with food; decrease of social interest; slowing of gastric emptying, giving feelings of fatness.

Reflections from Chapter 5

- What have I learned?

_____

_____

_____

_____

_____

_____

- How can I put what I have learned into practice?

_____

_____

_____

_____

_____

_____

_____

- What can I do differently as a result of reading this chapter?

_____

_____

_____

_____

_____

_____

_____

_____

6

How can Anorexia Nervosa be treated?

The earlier Anorexia Nervosa is recognised and treated, the quicker and less painful the route to recovery. Delay in recognition can lead to the condition becoming more severe and therefore requiring more intensive and long-term treatment. It is a feature of the condition that individuals with Anorexia Nervosa are initially vehemently opposed to acknowledging that there is a problem and are therefore reluctant to ask for help. Thus, the average delay between onset of the disorder and its treatment is five years. Effective treatment focuses on helping the individual to take responsibility for their own eating habits, and so depends on the willingness of the person with Anorexia Nervosa to accept help. This is why forcing the issue, and strong-arming a person with Anorexia Nervosa into treatment, is unlikely to be successful.

If treatment is never sought, some individuals will develop a very severe form of Anorexia Nervosa that is resistant to all forms of treatment currently available. Such cases require prolonged and intensive treatment and care. In the one long-term follow-up study published to date, some people recovered even after twelve years of continuous symptoms; but for those who suffered for longer than twelve years, no such recovery occurred. These latter remained either chronic sufferers or died as a result of the disorder. In the light of this finding, it is clear that speed is of the essence when it comes to tackling the disorder.

Initial steps to recovery

- The first and most important step is for the person with Anorexia Nervosa to acknowledge that there is *a problem*. Recognition of being severely under-weight is the vital first stage.

- The second step is to acknowledge the disorder, to the extent that there is a *willingness to ask for help*. This may be a parent or close friend, but in many cases the person with Anorexia Nervosa may be more comfortable seeking outside, professional help.

- Third, there must be a letting go of severe dietary restrictions. This will relieve the effects of severe starvation and begin to loosen the bonds of obsession with food intake. Initially the move towards regular eating may be pitifully small, but it is a critically important change.

Specialist treatment services

When seeking treatment for Anorexia Nervosa, the best

place to begin is with the GP. Most people with Anorexia Nervosa may be successfully treated as outpatients, using some form of psychological therapy. This may be undertaken by a clinical psychologist or nurse therapist. Usually there will be one principal therapist who will see the patient most frequently and liaise between the GP, psychiatrist or clinical psychologist, and other health professionals. Someone seeking help with Anorexia Nervosa is likely to come into contact with a range of professionals, all with their own particular areas of expertise, working in association with one another. The following are the practitioners most likely to be involved in treating a person with Anorexia Nervosa.

General practitioner (GP)

The GP or family doctor is usually the first professional with whom the person with Anorexia Nervosa will come into contact. In many cases, the individual will present to the GP with a condition secondary to the disorder, such as depression, cessation of menstruation or constipation. The GP will take a detailed history of the condition, which will lead to a diagnosis of the patient as suffering from Anorexia Nervosa. The stage to which the disorder has progressed will determine whether the doctor decides to refer the patient on to more specialist services or conduct the treatment at the GP surgery.

In cases where the disorder is not greatly advanced, the doctor may choose to manage the patient within the practice. This may involve a nurse therapist, who can provide basic nutritional and health education and referral of the individual to a local self-help group. This can be useful in providing information – such as resources and services that are available, including national eating disorder groups, books and dietary advice services – and assisting the acceptance and treatment of the disorder. This may provide a certain degree of comfort, as some people with Anorexia Nervosa are unaware that they are suffering from a recognised condition and that their thinking is distorted. The individual will be encouraged to see the problem as a psychological one, involving a response, albeit a maladaptive one, to stress or low self-esteem, rather than as one of being in the grip of a slimming or exercise disorder. If marked improvement is not made or the condition continues to worsen, the GP will refer the patient to a specialist.

Physician

The physician may be involved in confirming the diagnosis of Anorexia Nervosa, through the administration of simple but thorough tests analysing blood and bone density. The physician will also undertake checks aimed at excluding other physical origins for the marked weight loss, such as diabetes or endocrine disorders.

Clinical psychologist

The clinical psychologist also assesses and diagnoses the patient, but their primary means of treatment is psychological rather than pharmacological. They may offer group or individual therapy, or a combination of both.

Psychiatrist

The primary role of the psychiatrist is in the assessment and diagnosis of the patient's condition. Once this is done, a decision will be made on what form of treatment is best. The psychiatrist may choose to treat the patient or refer on to a therapist. Some people are strongly opposed to the idea of taking drugs as part of their treatment; they may be advised to request treatment by a therapist or clinical psychologist, who will not prescribe drugs.

Psychotherapist

A psychotherapist uses long-term exploratory work, usually within a psychodynamic framework. This can involve exploring the patient's past and uncovering the initial factors contributing to the development of Anorexia Nervosa. In this form of therapy, the therapist takes an interpretative rather than a directive role, thus allowing the patient to lead the session and explore issues with which he or she is concerned.

Dietician

The dietician's role is to assess dietary intake, and to educate the person with Anorexia Nervosa on the need for a balanced and healthy diet that will provide sufficient nutrients and calories for recovery. They will also encourage the consumption of an expanded range of foods. This is particularly important, as people with Anorexia Nervosa tend to subsist on an ever-smaller range of foods that they deem 'safe'. This may come about because they have a 'bad' experience with a particular foodstuff, perhaps because it makes them feel bloated and therefore 'fat', or because they rule out more and more foods on account of an unacceptably high calorie content. Expanding the food range helps to dismantle some of the fear and distrust of food.

Dieticians also encourage the use of food diaries, which they will then assess, going through them with the person under treatment. They may see the individual for a one-off treatment, or for a series of time-limited sessions.

Paediatrician

Children as young as six have been found to be preoccupied with body shape, weight and dietary behaviours, and there have been reports of an increasing number of pre-pubescent cases of Anorexia Nervosa. Paediatricians are therefore becoming increasingly aware, when dealing with children who show signs of weight loss or poor physical development, that such symptoms may be indicative of juvenile Anorexia Nervosa.

Art therapist

Art therapy can be especially helpful where a patient is

struggling to express feelings of frustration or pain. It may be used in conjunction with other forms of treatment, or as an independent therapy. It is a welcome alternative to more traditional therapies and can be useful in illuminating important issues.

Occupational therapist

The occupational therapist uses a variety of strategies, including projective art, relaxation, anxiety management, assertiveness training and psychodrama. A programme will be devised to suit the individual patient. For instance, body-oriented exercises may be used to correct body-image disturbances, which are particularly characteristic of Anorexia Nervosa.

Principles of comprehensive treatment

Any soundly based programme of treatment for Anorexia Nervosa will have three core objectives:

1. To increase weight so that it is within the normal range. This is the priority; only when this has been achieved can physiological functions resume their normal operation.
2. To help the individual re-establish normal eating patterns and to avoid extreme weight-control measure such as vomiting, laxative abuse or excessive exercising.
3. To explain the physical symptoms caused by Anorexia Nervosa.

Where there is a state of malnutrition or starvation, this is treated as a priority. Starvation is known to have profound effects psychologically as well as physically and can seriously hinder the efficacy of other types of treatment. Some form of psychological treatment is then seen as essential to confront underlying personal, interpersonal and social factors believed to foster and maintain the disorder. This may involve supportive psychotherapy, counselling about eating and dangerous purging habits and, where appropriate, other supports including relaxation, family therapy and marital therapy.

The treatment programme is multidimensional, with emphasis on different forms of treatment at different stages of the disorder. One person (the primary therapist) will be the main coordinator to whom the patient can relate and through whom other health professionals liaise.

Of primary importance once weight is at a safe level is the teaching of normal eating patterns. It is important that the individual takes control of their diet as soon as possible and, with support, begins to manage a more normal dietary intake.

Drugs are seldom necessary but may be useful if there are complicating additional medical problems or depression.

Hospitalisation and inpatient treatment

Treatment as a hospital inpatient is the most intensive form of intervention that may be offered to a person with Anorexia Nervosa. Cases where hospitalisation may be necessary include the following.

- Those in which weight loss has reached an extreme degree (usually defined by a body mass index below 13.5 kg/m2). In these circumstances the sense of helplessness felt both by the person with Anorexia Nervosa and by the family can often be relieved by an intervention to break the cycle. Even so, whether hospitalisation is appropriate is unlikely to depend on absolute weight alone; several other factors would usually also be considered: for example, the rate of weight loss, the severity of starvation symptoms and the degree of inflexibility on the part of the person with Anorexia Nervosa.
- Those in which other disorders or associated symptoms, such as depression, self-harm, suicide attempts, obsessional symptoms, diabetes or severe purging behaviour also occur.

Inpatient treatment is often a lengthy process, lasting for six to twelve months; it is intensive and aims to bring about both weight gain and changes in behaviour and attitude.

Hospital outpatient treatment and re-feeding

Hospital treatment as an outpatient is a more convenient and less disruptive form of help. It involves regular attendance as a day-patient for a combination of treatments that may include individual and group therapy, dietary advice, education and social activity. There is an expectation that eating is involved, at least in the form of one communal meal, and food shopping and food preparation are included.

One or perhaps two meals are supervised, and participants usually attend on five days a week for as long as necessary. The advantages of outpatient treatment are that the person with Anorexia Nervosa can gain weight at their own speed, and so can feel safe and in control. Responsibility can then be taken for eating and, with the support and encouragement of a therapist and dietician, a relearning of eating patterns can occur. This maintenance of the individual's sense of autonomy is very valuable, and though weight gain is usually slow in outpatients, there are pronounced behavioural and attitudinal changes that are sustained for longer periods after discharge than with inpatient treatment.

Drug treatment

Drugs play a relatively small part in the treatment of Anorexia Nervosa and are seldom used as the primary form of treatment. No drugs will directly affect the course of the illness, though some may be used to relieve certain symptoms: for example, antidepressants may be given to a patient also suffering from depression, just as antibiotics would be given to someone who has an infection. If drugs are used, it is as just one component of a wider treatment programme.

Family therapy

For those under sixteen, involvement of the family in therapy is recommended. Beyond sixteen it is up to the individual whether they wish to involve family members or not. From our clinical work, we have found that working with the family and the adult with Anorexia Nervosa can be very helpful and sometimes working with two families together can be even more beneficial.

Cognitive behavioural therapy

Cognitive behavioural therapy (CBT) is a form of short-term psychotherapy. Aaron Beck, the father-figure of cognitive therapy, coined the term 'collaborative empiricism' to describe the nature of the therapeutic enterprise where an individual, closely assisted by a therapist, investigates the basis in reality for a personal hypothesis concerning the world. In other words, both the therapist and the person undergoing therapy examine the truths on which the latter's worldview is based. It is a very rational form of therapy, in that it guides the individual towards a realistic view of their situation by examining facts rather than feelings.

CBT is not about the therapist arguing with the individual. It is about encouraging the individual to collect evidence that may support or refute their beliefs, and then re-evaluating those beliefs in the light of empirical evidence.

CBT and Anorexia Nervosa: an introduction

A central characteristic of standard cognitive behavioural therapy is its structured, time-limited framework, with each session directed by a previously planned agenda. This can suit the frame of mind typical of the person with Anorexia Nervosa, who tends to be most comfortable with order and a tight control of events. Cognitive behavioural therapy is non-historical in nature – that is, it deals with the present and uses a scientific methodology. These two features often appeal to people with Anorexia Nervosa who are not prepared to delve deep into the past, perhaps because they are not yet ready to face certain deep-rooted issues but *are* ready to deal with their disorder.

The individual and therapist work together to identify particular problem areas; for instance, the individual's belief that they are fat. In their own time, the individual embarks on a fact-finding mission regarding this area. These facts are then used to challenge the negative thought patterns that have arisen, using the cognitive skills learned in the therapeutic sessions. An important feature of CBT is its open nature, encouraging the individual to view treatment as a series of stages without a pass/fail definition.

Mood, behaviour and thoughts can all affect each other, and in the mind of the person with Anorexia Nervosa this can result in a vicious circle, as follows: a predominant belief in your own fatness can affect mood, making you feel low and panicky, which can affect behaviour, making you withdraw from other people, which means that your belief in your own fatness is never challenged, thereby affecting mood and so on. The circular entanglement of mood, thought and behaviour is illustrated in Figure 6.1.

Figure 6.1: Mood, thought and behaviour: the vicious circle

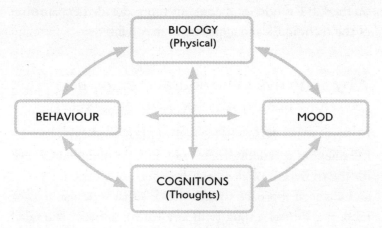

During CBT, the person is introduced to this concept and reveals the negative, self-defeating thoughts. These are often automatic and may rarely be held up to the light for examination. Such thoughts might include: '*People are staring at me because I am so fat!*' This thought would be described as a result of a preoccupation with body shape and weight. Discussion would also cover how the presence of this thought influences mood and behaviour. Thinking distortions would also be examined. For instance, the belief that: '*If I lose weight, all my problems will be solved*' is a common thinking distortion in people with Anorexia Nervosa and a dangerous one, as it allows the disorder to maintain its grip. CBT is used to challenge distortions such as these, which have become rooted in the mind, by seeking rational alternatives.

The self-help manual in Part Two of this book is based on the CBT model, and contains more detailed explanation of the techniques and approaches involved.

Why cognitive behavioural therapy as a psychological model for Anorexia Nervosa?

In May 2017, NICE published clinical guidelines for the treatment of eating disorders, which recommended CBT-E for the treatment of *all* eating disorders for adults. CBT-E is an enhanced approach (hence the 'E') that is designed to be used in a clinical setting with any eating disorder and takes what is commonly known as a *transdiagnostic approach* to treatment. What this essentially means is that the treatment is designed to treat the Eating Disorder, whether it is Anorexia Nervosa, Bulimia Nervosa or Binge Eating Disorder. This book, *Overcoming Anorexia Nervosa*, has used a traditional CBT approach and specifically addresses Anorexia Nervosa. CBT-E is a personalised clinical intervention and, just like our approach, it is specifically designed to address the factors that maintain the presenting difficulties.

Reflections from Chapter 6

- What have I learned?

_____

_____

_____

_____

_____

_____

- How can I put what I have learned into practice?

_____

_____

_____

_____

_____

_____

_____

- What can I do differently as a result of reading this chapter?

_____

_____

_____

_____

_____

_____

_____

_____

PART TWO

A SELF-HELP MANUAL

Introduction

*It occurred to me, slowly but surely, that I was missing
out. I was fifteen years old, I hadn't had a period in
over a year, and I never went out the house except to go
to school. I listened to music a lot and that sometimes
made me feel very sad, because the music was all about
people being in love and having relationships and I was
on the outside of it all. A year later, I was well on the
road to recovery, my weight had reached nearly seven
stones and my skin was beginning to look healthy. I
remember the morning I went to the toilet and discovered that I was having a period. I bet there can't be
many sixteen-year-old girls who literally want to whoop
because they have to wear tampons again. I felt as if I
had come back to life.*

Jane

If you think you have or are developing Anorexia Nervosa,
the very fact that you are reading this book is positive. It
shows that you have recognised that you may be experiencing problems in your approach to eating and body image
and that you want to address those problems. Getting from

A to B is not easy, but you are probably aware of that already. The important thing at this stage is that you are thinking about changing.

To motivate yourself now, and as you progress, think of the reasons why you want to change. It could be simply that you feel so unhappy that you believe any state would be better than this one. However, if you allow yourself to think about your situation more closely, you may be surprised at how many positive reasons there are to change. Maybe you feel lonely and know that without Anorexia Nervosa you would be better able to re-establish social contact. It could be that you avoid relationships with the opposite sex because you feel disgust at the thought of your own body but wish to overcome that; or you might do the opposite and find that you seek out what might be considered to be unhealthy relationships in order to try to gain approval and a sense of self-worth. It may be you would like to take on a new job or course of study, or pick up an old hobby again, but are prevented from doing so by the demands that Anorexia Nervosa makes on your time and energy.

Take time now to list the benefits of change and try to create some kind of mental picture of how you would like to be. Often, pinpointing exactly where you would like to end up makes it easier to get there. It is important to make changes at a pace that is manageable for you, which will probably involve pushing beyond your comfort zone at times, but needs to be balanced with not setting too many goals too quickly.

Step 1

Assessing the problem

Although it may be challenging, it is important to know that you CAN change your thoughts around food, eating and your body. This may not happen instantly – after all, developing Anorexia Nervosa is a gradual process – but it is possible.

It is also important to be aware that, if you have Anorexia Nervosa, you may have a tendency to make unreasonable demands of yourself. When following this self-help programme, bear this in mind, and consciously try NOT to criticise yourself when the going gets tough, or you feel that you have taken one step forward and two steps back. Congratulate yourself on every successful move forward and be easy on yourself for any slips; this is a natural part of the process and does not mean your situation is hopeless.

A key feature of this self-help programme is the diary templates printed at intervals through the manual. Extra copies are also printed at the back of the book, but you might want to photocopy these so that you have fresh pages at hand when you need them. It is also helpful to have a notebook for recording your progress as you go along, as well as for noting down your current state of mind, what you hope to achieve, and what your current patterns of eating and behaviour are. It is up to you whether you wish to share your written thoughts with anyone else, but it is important that you are honest with yourself and feel uninhibited about what you write. This is, first and foremost, a record for you.

The first steps: where are you now?

- The first step is to establish where you are now. Take time to read through the following points and write down your thoughts as they occur to you.

- Try to recall the things that prompted you to change your behaviour around food and eating in the first place.

- Were you overweight, or did you want to prove something to yourself or others, or assert your individuality? For instance, did you embark on a diet to 'just lose a bit of weight' or perhaps because you were told not to? Then ask yourself: why was the weight loss so successful? For instance, did the loss of weight give you such a sense of achievement that you wanted to keep it going?

- If you feel that Anorexia Nervosa has taken a hold of you, consider the things that may be maintaining it. Try to look at your situation dispassionately and be as truthful as you can. Your thoughts, and any notes you take, are for yourself and need not be shown to anyone else; so, do not feel vulnerable acknowledging that you have developed secretive habits or deceive others in order to keep your food intake low.

- Remember that the factors that are maintaining your Anorexia Nervosa may be quite different from the ones that triggered it in the first place. It will be very helpful to consider what these initial triggers were, but be aware that understanding these is not the solution in itself. Remember also that the trigger factors will be different for different people and likewise for the maintaining factors.

- Refer to an app to work out your body mass index; www.nhs.uk has the BMI healthy weight calculator, which is very easy to access and use.

- If you have been living on a severely reduced food intake for six months, your Anorexia Nervosa has become an illness, and you may be developing some of the physical symptoms described in Chapter 2. You may feel that you are locked into anorexic behaviour, that you are constantly weighing yourself, planning when and what to eat, and living an existence quite divorced from that of those around you. This is a very distressing stage of Anorexia Nervosa. You may feel extremely isolated and as if your view of your situation is the only accurate one.

- If your Anorexia Nervosa is more long-standing than this, or indeed recurring, the chances are that it has become a way of life for you. You may find it hard to imagine living without it and have lost interest in everything but your Anorexia Nervosa.

If you have put yourself in either of the last two categories, take time to consider what caused you to progress through and beyond the first two stages. Was it simply the passage of time, or did the onset of negative feelings or hopelessness reduce your self-confidence and make it hard for you to reverse the process? Or did you develop rituals and obsessions that gradually expanded to dominate your life?

_____

_____

_____

_____

_____

_____

_____

_____

_____

_____

_____

_____

_____

_____

Keep the notes you have made and add to them as new thoughts occur to you. You may be surprised by seeing it all written down in black and white, and the record may help you to monitor your state of mind in the future.

Most importantly, by tackling this first exercise, and thereby acknowledging that you are experiencing some difficulties, you have taken a giant step towards your recovery.

Should you seek professional help?

It is a sensible precaution to seek professional help if you have Anorexia Nervosa, if only to ensure as you embark on the self-help programme that your restricted food intake has not triggered any further medical complications. However, there are some situations in which it is particularly advisable that you consult professional medical practitioners.

- If your Anorexia Nervosa is of a bulimic nature, it is wise to have your heart and blood pressure checked regularly.
- It is particularly important for women who have ceased to menstruate to seek medical advice.
- You should also seek professional help if you are suffering from severe depression, either independent of or as a result of Anorexia Nervosa. The reason for this is that depressive illness may hinder any attempts on your part to improve your situation on your own, as it may rob you of the necessary motivation and self-belief that a self-help programme requires. A

doctor may offer you a range of treatment options that could help alleviate some of the depressive symptoms, including, but not limited to, antidepressant medication.

- You may wish to seek external help if you feel that you need support to make change and have no one in the family or close environment who can fulfil that role. In such cases a therapist, GP or support group may be able to help.

- Finally, if you find that, upon reading through the following steps in the programme, you instinctively react against the changes suggested, and find that you cannot counteract this instinct, do seek help.

Awareness of obstacles

It is only realistic to acknowledge that changing your thoughts and behaviour is not going to be easy. Reviewing the likely obstacles to change does not mean taking a negative or defeatist attitude: on the contrary, if you take a clear-sighted look at the ways in which resistance to change might affect you, you will be better prepared to deal with them if and when they arise, rather than taking them as reasons to give up.

Lack of commitment

If this self-help programme is to work, it is important to make a commitment to change. Initially this will seem alarming – even like stepping off a cliff into space – but in fact you are not stepping into the unknown. ***You have been free from Anorexia Nervosa before, and there is no reason why you cannot be again.***

Be aware of any tendency to procrastinate and try to stop yourself from reasoning yourself out of making the change now. There will be no time that seems exactly right, so commit yourself to beginning, and stick with that commitment. Keeping a diary, as described below, can help to reinforce commitment; in the following steps of the programme you will learn techniques to counteract your wavering, and be able to record your use of them and build on them.

Fear of losing control

The chances are that your life is completely organised around your Anorexia Nervosa. In a sense, although you may feel that Anorexia Nervosa gives you a way of exercising control, it is your Anorexia Nervosa that has taken over the reins and is controlling you. What you are seeking to do now is to regain genuine control for yourself – even though at times it may not seem that way as you will be faced with challenges that are difficult to overcome and will have to break your previous strict patterns of rigorous self-control. Try to keep to the forefront of your mind the essential fact that you are not relinquishing control but restoring it to yourself. Currently, it is not you who are in control – your Anorexia Nervosa is.

Fear of change

All major life changes can be terrifying – even the positive ones, such as having a child or getting a promotion at work – and yet without change, our lives stultify. The fear of change may be especially strong because, perhaps, you find it difficult to conceive that it will make you anything other than more unhappy than you currently are. Challenge this thought as it occurs. Even when it is hard to believe, the truth is that you will be happier once you have made changes and realised that you have the ability to overcome your fears. Following this programme and combating your Anorexia Nervosa is one of the most positive and rewarding changes you will ever make in your life.

Isolation

Anorexia Nervosa works in a very insidious way, and isolates the person suffering from it. If your Anorexia Nervosa is reasonably advanced, you may already have withdrawn from social relationships and feel that you have become separated even from close friends and family. However, you are less alone than you think. Those around you may seem distant, but much of this is to do with the fact that they do not know how to approach you and are frustrated by their seeming inability to help. If you crave support, ask for it. If it is not available close at hand, then seek it from professional services or from an eating disorder support group. Not only will this take you out of your isolation; you will find that you are not the only person in the world to be dominated by anorexic thoughts, and not the only person seeking to be free from them.

Self-defeating mechanisms

Be aware of the fact that your Anorexia Nervosa is not going to give up without a fight. You have probably already developed a complex system of thought that is hard to break free from, and one aspect of this is a tendency to tell yourself you are not capable of change. Avoid interpreting every setback as proof that you cannot achieve change. Think of the example of a smoker, who quits entirely for three months and then, one night at a party, smokes five cigarettes. Is that single occasion proof that the person is incapable of quitting and should therefore just give in and return to smoking regularly? Of course it is not, and most would-be ex-smokers will recognise this. Learn to concentrate on your successes and count them as proof of your ability to change. Self-defeating mechanisms can themselves be defeated; all you need to do is recognise them for what they are.

Developing motivation for change: the pros and cons of Anorexia Nervosa

It is important to remember that Anorexia Nervosa may have helped to solve many of your problems. You didn't develop Anorexia Nervosa because you are crazy, neurotic or self-indulgent. You developed it because it was a solution to many of your problems or feelings that were present before the Anorexia Nervosa started. Looking at the advantages of anorexia may help you understand why it developed and why it may be so hard to consider giving it up.

Make a detailed list of all the advantages of having Anorexia Nervosa. Don't be defensive about this. Remember that developing this was an adaptive solution to your problems at the time. Always start with the advantages first; then make a list of all the disadvantages. It is likely that at this stage the pros will outweigh the cons. If this is the case, don't panic. It merely emphasises that Anorexia Nervosa was an adaptive and understandable solution for you. If you find it difficult to do this exercise, enrol the help of a trusted friend or relative. Ask them what they see as the advantages and disadvantages for you. Again, urge them to be open and honest.

What to do with the pros and cons list

First, simply making the list may help you look differently at your current situation. Maybe writing down all the disadvantages will help you realise how hard it is to maintain the Anorexia Nervosa. The list will give you lots of experiments you can do using the cognitive techniques described later in this book. Take each statement in turn and look at it in detail. Rephrase each statement as a question – for example, 'Does starvation really improve my mood?' – and then test it out over a few days, keeping note of what evidence you find.

Projecting into the future

Perhaps it is the case that the advantages clearly outweigh the disadvantages just now. Try imagining what it would be like in one year's, two years', five years' or ten years' time. A good way of doing this is to imagine a meeting with a close friend who doesn't have Anorcxia Nervosa. At each meeting, imagine that you are the same, and that you have to say what you've been doing and what has been happening in your life since the last meeting. Then turn things around and imagine what he or she might say. If you cannot do this on your own, try it for real, with a close friend. Sometimes it is only when you can look five or ten years ahead and see how much of life you may have missed out on because of Anorexia Nervosa that it will really come home to you that you do need to change. For example, in ten years' time you might still be saying, '*Well, I've still got Anorexia Nervosa; I'm still very thin; I'm still in control; it is still a battle every day; I haven't formed any new close relationships; I never completed college. My life revolves around food and restricting.*'

Table: Advantages and disadvantages of Anorexia Nervosa

Advantages	Disadvantages
1. I feel in control of myself and my body this way.	1. Although I don't eat, I think about food all the time. It's exhausting.
2. No one can think I am indulgent or greedy when I look this way.	2. I have cravings about food which are hard to control.
3. People take more notice of me, I get compliments and attention.	3. I am terrified that I might binge.
4. I can wear clothes that I never dreamt I would be able to wear.	4. I am cold all the time, even in the summer.
5. Things in my family have changed. They show me concern rather than ignore me now.	5. At times I feel exhausted and weak.
6. When I starve, my mood improves.	6. I am missing out on my old social life because I cannot eat with others.
7. My self-esteem is better.	7. I am more irritable.
8. I have much more confidence.	8. My sleep is disturbed.
9. My body no longer feels disgusting.	9. My concentration gets bad, particularly at the end of the day.

10. I feel pure and clean.	10. My skin is dry and itchy.
11. My sex drive has disappeared.	11. I worry about my fertility.
12. I can concentrate on work and don't have to bother with food.	12. I worry about my bones.
13. The thinness protects me from close relationships.	13. I have become even more preoccupied about my body and shape.
14. If I have Anorexia Nervosa I get psychotherapy.	14. I feel guilty about being this way; it is self-indulgent.
15. I can run easily, I don't have to train any more.	15. I cause my family a great deal of worry and stress.
16. My periods have stopped.	16. I have to keep going to the doctor.
17. Men pay me less attention. If they do show interest it is concern.	17. I am terrified I may end up in hospital.
18. I feel independent and free this way.	18. It is such an effort; can I keep going this way?
	19. My mood crashes for no reason.

Writing a letter to your Anorexia Nervosa

If you do finally decide to change, giving up Anorexia Nervosa will not be easy. You may go through a period of grief or a sense of loss, as the Anorexia Nervosa may have served you well over a number of years. One way of coping with this is to write a letter to your Anorexia as though it were a friend you are saying goodbye to and will never see again. Write about all the good times you have had together, what you will miss, and how you will cope without it. This exercise might help you distance yourself from your Anorexia Nervosa so that you come to regard it as something that is separate from you, rather than an integral part of you.

It might also be useful when you have written the letter to do something symbolic with it, such as put it in an envelope, seal it up and put it away, or burn it. Sometimes keeping the letter and re-reading it may be helpful. The following is an example of a letter written by a patient of mine who eventually decided to change after ten years of severe Anorexia Nervosa.

Dear Anorexia Nervosa

I am sorry that we have to part. You have been my best, most loyal and most trusted friend for the past ten years. You have never let me down, always been there for me, and I could always turn to you when I was most distressed.

No one else has stood by me like you, day in day out, year after year.

I don't know how I will cope without you, but I am determined to try. I feel very frightened about not being able to turn to you in future. I also feel angry with you. I thought that I could control you, but gradually you came to control me. You never left me alone; even when I thought I was coping without you, you tormented me and tricked me back into your grasp. At times I really hate you for what you have done to my life. Maybe I will cope without you. I am certainly going to try. I want you out of my life. I want you separate from me, I want peace from you; leave me alone.

I'll miss you.

Love, Sarah

Coping with your family and your friends

In many cases, this section might be better entitled 'The family and friend's guide to coping with you'. The idea is to encourage you to do some preparatory work, including considering a number of questions about your close relationships, before you move on to the next step of the programme. In this way you can start to change your environment in such a way as to support you better as you set about making changes in your behaviour and attitudes.

- First of all, read again the section entitled 'Family structure' in Chapter 5.
- Next, read through and answer the questions below in 'Assessing the relationship of your Anorexia

Nervosa to your family'. Note that these questions do not have correct or incorrect answers; they are designed to start you thinking about your Anorexia Nervosa in the context of your home and family life.

- Finally, work out a plan, either alone or with your family, to cover the areas you wish to tackle.

Assessing the relationship of your Anorexia Nervosa to your close relationships

Consider what would change for the positive within your close relationships if your Anorexia Nervosa disappeared this instant.

- Would tension be reduced? That is, would there be fewer arguments or potential arguments?
- Would you be able to eat meals together?
- Would your parents, siblings, partner, children be less anxious about you? Or less frustrated with you?
- Would you be able to enjoy activities together?
- Would the closeness in your relationships improve?
- Are there any other changes that would be positive?

Now consider what negative changes might occur if your Anorexia Nervosa did not exist. If you cannot think of any, cast your mind back to the first few weeks and months of your Anorexia Nervosa and try to remember the differences between then and now.

- Did your members of your family show more interest in you? And would that interest diminish if your Anorexia Nervosa disappeared?
- Did you get to have things your own way? And would you return to not having things your own way?
- Did you/do you enjoy playing the 'sick role', and being regarded as incapable of doing certain things and in need of extra care? Would the relinquishing of that role distress you?
- Are there any other changes that would be negative?

Formulating a plan of action

The actual process of formulating a plan can be of enormous benefit, particularly for those close to you, who may feel frustrated and helpless in the face of Anorexia Nervosa. It is important to be assertive when formulating this plan; allowing yourself to be bamboozled into doing what others want may only exacerbate your condition by increasing the desire to assert control over your life through food. The plan can include concrete goals in the short, medium and long term.

Use your answers from the assessment above to help you. For instance, if you feel that one of the positive aspects of not having Anorexia Nervosa would be being able to have meals with your family, then this should be written down as an aim. Discuss this issue with your family, and set yourself a target of, perhaps, sitting down with them to one meal per week. At first, you may be unable to eat exactly as your family do, but keep in mind that this is what you are working towards. Perhaps they could meet you halfway, by eating a meal that you could comfortably share.

Though it may seem a little scary at first, it can be a tremendous relief to engage with your family in this way, and to allow them to help you loosen your self-control – and your isolation.

If you found that one of the negative aspects of being free from Anorexia Nervosa was that you would receive less attention from your family, then request the time to discuss this with them. Do other family members feel this way? Is yours a family in which only negative behaviour and events get attention, while good things are ignored? If so, try to think of ways in which the focus can be turned towards the positive. Instead of emphasising where problems lie, try emphasising the good aspects of situations, focusing on achievements and successes.

When implementing a plan of action, try to approach it in a reasonably business-like way. Take it seriously and take note of its progress. It is unlikely to go 100 per cent smoothly, and you may suffer setbacks, but don't let this put you back at square one. The very fact that you are involving your family is a step forward, and you may make unexpected leaps and bounds as they become more involved.

_____

_____

_____

_____

_____

_____

_____

_____

_____

_____

_____

Anorexia Nervosa as a weapon

Some people may find that Anorexia Nervosa feels like a weapon or a suit of armour. It may be that the family focuses on the negatives, as described above, and that you feel that you have been consistently ignored in favour of siblings/relatives/parents who are ill (or in trouble or in distress). In some cases, this can result in a sibling developing Anorexia Nervosa in response to another family member's Anorexia Nervosa.

Alternatively, you may feel that you are (or have been) expected to conform to a family pattern, such as high academic achievement, and you developed the illness as a way of declaring your individuality and rebelling against constraining expectations.

If you feel that your Anorexia Nervosa is in some way a weapon, it is important to establish, even if only in your own mind, why this is so. If you want to broach the issue with your family but feel that they won't listen to you, or simply that you don't know how to begin talking to them about such issues, then family therapy may help. A family therapist can act as an intermediary, helping you and your family to articulate how you feel and assisting in negotiation.

As in relation to obstacles generally, awareness of the factors affecting your close relationships is extremely important and can be a vital first step in tackling Anorexia Nervosa. The next stage is to act on it rather than hide behind your Anorexia Nervosa. However angry or impotent you feel, you are only treading water emotionally if you stop here.

Anorexia Nervosa and other relationships

Anorexia Nervosa can be enormously destructive to relationships outside as well as within the family, whether with friends or partners. It can halt any kind of natural development in partnerships, and make the partner feel very hopeless and isolated. Many people with Anorexia Nervosa find that, due to a chronically poor self-image, they become reluctant to engage in a sexual relationship. Naturally, this can be devastating for the partner.

One of the most destructive effects of Anorexia Nervosa on a relationship is that the partner may feel responsible and is almost certain to feel in the dark. This can result in disputes about eating and weight, which have little effect other than to put further strain on the relationship and increase the sense of need for perceived control.

The first step here is to speak with your partner, as far as you are able. Explaining how you feel and why you are driven to restrict food intake to such an extent will ease some of the strain; setting ground rules, such as requesting that your eating patterns are not interfered with, can go some way to re-establishing links. If your partner feels uncomfortable discussing your Anorexia Nervosa, which can happen if they are fearful or reluctant to acknowledge the existence of the disorder, then a therapist who can talk to you both may be helpful.

When you are ready to make changes, enlist your partner's support. Not surprisingly, they are usually more than happy to help. The important thing is to make it clear at what rate you intend to make these changes, and that you should not be criticised when you lapse. Above all, keep open the lines of dialogue.

We had reached a stalemate. My partner asking for
sex, and my avoiding it. Occasionally this would erupt
into a confrontation, and I could see that he felt hurt
and rejected, but he couldn't see that, as I lost more and

more weight, I felt increasingly disgusted with my body and found the thought of intimacy unbearable. I did try to explain how I felt but he didn't want to hear it. He would listen in stony silence and say nothing. I began to realise that he was frightened of the idea that I wasn't 'normal' or that somehow, he was 'defective'.

When I asked my GP to refer me to a therapy group, I told my partner, but he seemed uninterested. He would drive me to the group, wait outside for me, and drive me home, all the time saying nothing.

After a few weeks, he wanted to know why I wasn't getting better!

The breakthrough, such as it was, came in fits and starts. I was learning assertiveness techniques, and how to articulate what was happening with me, through talking to other people with Anorexia Nervosa. It began with me making long, rambling speeches and him listening, silently. Finally, I asked him to help me by reading through my plan of action. I wanted to stop thinking along anorexic lines, and to do so meant that I had to face the fact that weight gain was necessary. I told him that I found the idea frightening, and that I needed someone to reassure me. He promised to help me. Though he found it awkward and would refer to the difficulties I was having as 'the problem', we did start to feel more at ease with each other, and my Anorexia stopped being something that kept us at arm's length and began almost to be something that made us closer.

Angela

Reflections from Step 1

- What have I learned?

_____

_____

_____

_____

_____

_____

_____

- How can I put what I have learned into practice?

_____

_____

_____

_____

_____

_____

_____

- What can I do differently as a result of reading this chapter?

_____

_____

_____

_____

_____

_____

_____

Step 2

Monitoring your eating

- The next step after assessing the problem is to monitor your current eating patterns. It is important to do this before attempting to make any changes.
- Recovery from Anorexia Nervosa involves you learning to relax about eating and no longer being controlled by food and what you eat.
- Recovery involves *risk-taking* and *challenging* your previous patterns of eating.
- Change may seem daunting, even terrifying, but if you feel intimidated by the prospect of change, try to remember that this is a *fear* reaction to change and the best way to overcome that fear is to try to face it.

Keeping a food diary

The first concrete step is to make a note of everything that you eat and drink on a daily basis. One way to do this is to use the diary sheets provided here at the end of the book. If you have access to a photocopier, copy the blank sheets printed here and keep them together when you have filled them in.

Alternatively, you could buy a notebook and make a diary yourself, following a similar layout. It will help if your notebook is of a small, convenient size.

Many people use calorie-counting apps on their mobile phones, which, in our experience, are not helpful. If you have an app that you can record your food and *not* the calories, that would be a good one to try. The important point here is to find a way to record your intake on a daily basis that works for you.

You will see that the diary sheets have four columns to the right of the spaces where you will record what you eat and drink. The first column, headed 'Portion', is where you will record the number of portions you have eaten when you use the portion system outlined in Step 5; don't worry about this for now. You can record from the beginning in the appropriate columns when and how many times you vomit ('Vomit'), take laxatives ('Laxative') and/or exercise ('Exercise') after eating. You can also record in the wide left-hand column any binges you may have and what you consumed in them; these foods and drinks should be placed in brackets.

Try to keep your food diary up to date through the day rather than waiting until the evening. If you write down everything as soon as possible after eating and drinking, it will be easier to make sure the record is accurate. People take differently to diary writing. Some find it helps them feel in control and easily maintain a full, accurate diary, while others find it hard and time-consuming. If you find it difficult, try to focus your efforts on particular days: two

Table: A suggested food diary

	Portion	Vomit	Laxative	Exercise
Breakfast:				
Snack:				
Lunch:				
Snack:				
Evening meal:				
Snack:				
Totals:				

fully recorded days out of a week will be more valuable than a whole week of semi-completed days.

You may well find at first that your diary shows a very self-restrained diet and very definite patterns of 'allowed' foods. You may also notice how you use exercise after eating to 'work off' the meal. The next step is to try to make yourself more aware of, and to move towards, the principles of normal eating

Principles of healthy eating

The principles of healthy eating, shown below, are a set of targets towards which you should aim – not a set of rules that must be kept rigidly all at once. Your plan is to take steps towards healthy eating, testing out each new practice at a pace that is tolerable to you, even if this means that progress appears to be very slow. Remember, you are more likely to lose heart and give up if you try to be too ambitious too soon than if you persevere little by little and give yourself time to get used to different ways of eating.

Once you have managed to follow these guidelines for some time, you will then be in a much stronger position to make more substantial changes to your diet and eating patterns.

- If you can, try to eat in company, not alone.
- Do not do anything else while you eat (except socialising), even if you are bingeing. For instance, do not

144

watch TV or read. You can listen to music, especially if this helps you relax, but the important thing is that you should try to concentrate on enjoying your meal.

- Establish a regular eating pattern. Plan to eat three meals a day plus three snacks, at predetermined times, in the sequence:

Breakfast
Snack
Lunch
Snack
Dinner
Snack

Plan your meals so that you try to keep one step ahead of the problem.

It cannot be stressed too much that these principles are recommendations to aim for; it may be that you won't achieve them quickly or without taking risks and experimenting. The important thing is that you become aware of a different, healthier way of fitting food into your life.

Helpful tactics

There are various ways in which you can help yourself as you set out on your journey towards change. The task ahead of you is a hard one, so do take every opportunity to make it a little easier.

- Try to think of an activity you may enjoy doing that does not involve food (avoid cooking) or intense calorie-burning (avoid intense aerobic exercise). Examples could include drawing, painting, reading, learning a new language, pottery, visiting the cinema, colouring-in. It could be some activity you used to enjoy but have not participated in for years. Make time to do this.

- Identify triggers that are most likely to cause you to restrict food intake, using your recent experience and the evidence provided by your diary. Examples could include comments about your weight or eating habits, or a friend or relative starting a diet and eating less. Think through these situations and write them down, along with reasons why you think they should not affect you. Then you can refer to these later should any of the situations arise and tempt you to use food or behaviours as a way to cope.

- Thoughts around food will inevitably arise and that is OK. Try not to judge yourself when this happens but work towards letting these thoughts come and go as any other type of thought does. The idea is that you try not to let these thoughts go round and round unchallenged, if possible.

- If you have spent time reading recipes and cookbooks and internet/social media accounts, or have been cooking for the family and/or friends, try to wean yourself off these activities and fill your time differently (this will be easier if you have identified other activities, as suggested in the first point in this list).

- Try hard not to weigh yourself more than once a week. If possible, stop weighing yourself altogether by hiding your scales.

- If you suffer from the anxiety and depression that commonly accompany Anorexia Nervosa, remember that, over time, they will become less severe as you gain weight. However, if you can identify particular problems that are clearly getting you down, focus on them and try to do something positive towards solving or at least minimising them.

- If you are exercising, ask yourself what you get from it: if it is merely to burn calories, try to think of a sport or activity that is more fulfilling and that will give you more genuine satisfaction for its own sake.

- Do not worry if you have not had a period for some time, or indeed ever. When your body returns to a healthier weight, your periods will also return, symbolising that your whole body is starting to function properly again.

- Set aside some time daily to reflect on how you are coping. If some of your strategies are not working, try others.
- Set yourself limited, realistic and concrete goals; work from hour to hour rather than from day to day; one failure does not mean that a succession of failures will follow.
- Note your successes, however modest, in your diaries. Every time you eat healthily you are reinforcing your new good eating habits.

CHAPTER SUMMARY

- In order to begin to change, it is important to record your current eating and drinking patterns. A daily food diary is a good way to do this.
- It is also important to begin to become aware of, and to try to work towards, the principles of healthy eating.
- There are various ways in which you can make life easier for yourself as you embark on the self-help programme.

HOMEWORK ASSIGNMENT FOR STEP 2

- Use a food diary to monitor your eating patterns. You could use the diary sheet provided here or make up your own in a notebook or use an app (that doesn't count calories).

- Try to work on at least one of the 'principles of healthy eating' each week. Write it down in your notebook/app.

- At the end of each week, review your food diary and note any changes, positive or negative, in your eating patterns. Spend some time thinking about how these were brought about and whether you found them hard or easy to make.

- Try to put into practice some of the tactics suggested to make it easier for you to begin to change.

- If you find you are unable to keep up a diary, or to make any progress at all towards principles of healthy eating, don't worry; just go back to the beginning and try again. Remember, you wouldn't expect miracles from other people; so, don't expect them of yourself.

- Don't forget to reward yourself for any achievements you have made.

Reflections from Step 2

- What have I learned?

_____

_____

_____

_____

_____

_____

_____

- How can I put what I have learned into practice?

_____

_____

_____

_____

_____

_____

_____

- What can I do differently as a result of reading this chapter?

_____

_____

_____

_____

_____

_____

_____

Step 3

Challenging the way you think (1): automatic thoughts

How thinking affects behaviour

The diagram below shows how thoughts, biology, behaviour and mood are interrelated, and how a vicious circle can arise as a result – each element has an effect on the other.

Figure 3.1: The interrelation of thoughts, behaviour, biology and mood

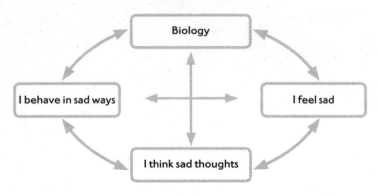

For instance, imagine you caught a cold. The physical effects that this has on you (biology) make you *feel* weak and apathetic. This in turn may make you *think* more negatively, e.g. 'I look so awful today – all pale and puffy faced. I'd better stay in.' The result of thinking this in turn affects your *behaviour* in that you stay inside longer. By staying in, you may get bored and start to feel more negative about yourself – and thus the cycle is perpetuated.

In the same way, a vicious circle is set up in Anorexia Nervosa. The effect of thinking about fat and how you ought to be thinner has a direct effect on your behaviour, prompting you to restrict, not take in enough nutrition, exercise, vomit, etc. These behaviours lead to restricting food intake and therefore trigger more thoughts about food and eating. This restrictive eating pattern also has a direct effect on your biology – it causes lack of concentration, sleep disturbance, irregular periods and so on – and often results in you feeling low in mood.

Can you think of any examples of vicious cycles like this affecting you? Write down some examples using the model contained in the diagram to make links between biology, behaviour, thinking and mood.

Figure 3.2: Effects of starvation on biology

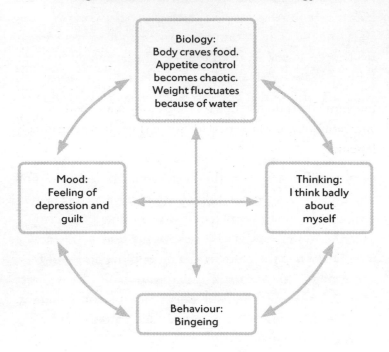

There are things that can help to improve your mood somewhat (social interaction, self-care, relaxation) and some medications may help by working on the biological symptoms of depression. One of the most positive impacts on changing mood is made by learning to think less negatively of yourself, your food and your weight. This will enable you to change your behaviour, introducing the principles of healthy eating, and thus to break out of the cycle. Cognitive behavioural therapy provides a way of doing this.

Anorexia Nervosa and distortions in thought

Anorexia Nervosa is an eating disorder that affects your mood and the way you think, feel, behave and interact in relationships. Even when the behavioural symptoms of Anorexia Nervosa have disappeared, and you are eating healthily, the anorexic thoughts or preoccupations with food, weight and eating can often persist for some time, before gradually lessening.

Figure 3.3: Anorexia Nervosa affects your behaviour, thoughts, mood and relationships

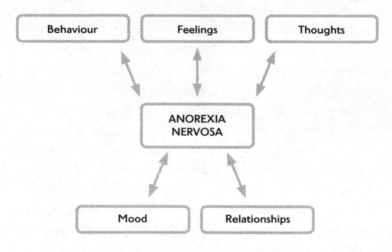

Typical thoughts include:

- People are staring at me because I'm so fat and gross.
- Everything will be all right when I lose some more weight.

- I must always exercise after eating to stop the calories turning to fat.
- I am a failure.
- I will never be good enough.
- If I don't eat by a certain time my day is ruined.

These thoughts may seem to make sense on the surface but are distorted and driven by the eating disorder, and are therefore not helpful to you as a person and your recovery. The issues around which they revolve may have come to preoccupy most, if not all your thoughts, so that you are unable to enjoy activities or concentrate on other things; in other words, they have come to dictate how you lead your life. These thoughts also impede progress because they represent arguments that encourage you to maintain your disordered eating.

Typically, someone with Anorexia Nervosa believes that they are the only person in the world who thinks and behaves as they do, but when they talk to others with Anorexia Nervosa they are amazed to find that there are many in exactly the same position.

Cognitive distortions – distortions in the way you think – don't just affect you. If you think in this way, you will have a negative view not only of yourself, but of the future and of the world around you.

What CBT can do to help you

Cognitive behavioural therapy is aimed at helping you *learn to recognise unhelpful thinking styles that prevent you from changing your behaviour.* By using this manual, which is based on a cognitive behavioural approach, you will:

- Learn to apply your reasoning skills to situations you find to be difficult, in particular those related to your eating.
- Learn to find alternative ways of thinking that will help you to change your behaviour and make you feel better.
- Be encouraged to think of yourself as a scientist, testing out or experimenting with your ideas to find out how realistic or helpful they are, by choosing practical tests to undertake at each stage of the programme.

Understanding automatic thoughts

Having automatic thoughts is normal. Everyone has them, and they can be considered to be good, bad or indifferent. We all have thoughts running through our minds the whole time, although we are not always conscious of what we are actually thinking. Nor do we normally question our own thinking; therefore, even if it becomes excessively negative or self-critical, we tend just to believe that the thoughts are factual. However, how one thinks about oneself can be very strongly affected by all sorts of factors, such as life circumstances, self-confidence, body image, etc.

If you have Anorexia Nervosa, you probably have powerful automatic thoughts that come into play to prompt you to avoid eating or exercise excessively. This step supports you to recognise and counter automatic thoughts. First of all, though, it is important to understand what an automatic thought is.

Characteristics of automatic thoughts

- They are automatic: they are not actually arrived at on the basis of reason or logic, but just seem to happen. It can help to think of them as part of the running commentary on life that goes on inside our heads almost constantly while we are awake.
- They are our own interpretations of what is going on around us, rather than facts. They depend on all sorts of factors, such as our level of self-confidence and how things are going in our lives generally. If we feel confident and happy, then the automatic thoughts we have are likely to reflect this by being positive and optimistic; however, if we feel unhappy and low in confidence, the automatic thoughts are likely to be negative and pessimistic.
- Negative automatic thoughts are often unreasonable and serve no useful purpose. They are based on an individual's view of themselves and often do not coincide with reality. Even if they are not actually irrational, they make you feel worse. They can prevent you from getting better by persuading you that there is no point in trying to change, even before you

have tried to do so. They may allow you to justify putting things off. 'There is no point in my working through this manual; I'll be wasting my time: I've had Anorexia Nervosa for so long, I must be a hopeless case.'

- Even though these thoughts may be unreasonable and/or unhelpful to you, they probably seem very believable at the time when you actually think them, and because they are automatic it is very unlikely that you are able to stand back from them and evaluate or question them. The nature of automatic thoughts means you are likely to accept them as easily as an ordinary automatic thought such as '*I should answer the door*' when the doorbell rings.

Recording negative automatic thoughts

The next step is to identify and record your negative thoughts in your diary. If you start to feel bad for any reason, take a step back and try to review your thoughts. Try to catch exactly what has just passed through your mind. These are the thoughts to write down; they can be seen as your automatic reactions, either to something that has just happened or to an issue that you have been thinking about, such as your Anorexia Nervosa. You will probably find that these thoughts are:

- often negative;
- believable;

- just pop into mind with no effort;
- unhelpful;
- universal;
- frequent;
- intense.

It is important to try to recognise some negative thoughts of your own. Below is an excerpt from the cognitive therapy diary of a twenty-one-year-old student who had suffered from Anorexia Nervosa for four years. This may help you to identify some of your own negative automatic thoughts. If so, jot them down in a blank diary page. *Don't worry* if none come to mind immediately. You will have a chance over the next week to add some to your food diary.

The typical automatic thoughts of a person suffering from an eating disorder tend to be preoccupied with food, weight and shape and self-worth. Some further examples are:

- *If I lose a stone, my life will be OK.*
- *I feel ashamed of my figure. If I was slim, people would like me more.*
- *I'm no use – I'm so fat and ugly, I have no control of my life. When she said, 'You look well', she meant, 'You look fat.'*
- *It's not worth living if I get any fatter than this.*
- *I'll never be the person I want to be.*
- *I'm just not being good enough.*
- *I'm not loved.*

- *I must be a bad person.*
- *I am just letting everyone down.*

Below is an example of a diary entry that has captured the *Situation* (what, where and when), the *Emotions* (described in one word) and the *Automatic Thoughts*.

Sample diary 2: Challenging automatic thoughts

Date	Emotions	Situation	Automatic Thoughts
12.05.17	Disgust. Anger.	Sitting alone in my room after eating some chocolate.	I must not eat anything tomorrow to make up for the pig-out I had tonight.
14.05.17	Fear. Panic.	Sitting in the dining room at lunchtime.	People are staring at me because they know I have Anorexia.
15.05.17	Ashamed. Miserable.	In a department store trying on a dress.	If I can't fit that dress I must be overweight. I look so fat in this dress, I may as well go home.

Diary 2: Challenging automatic thoughts

Date	Emotions	Situation	Automatic Thoughts

CHAPTER SUMMARY

- Anorexia Nervosa affects not just the way you behave but also the way you think.
- Preoccupations with food, weight and eating often remain even once the *behavioural* symptoms of Anorexia Nervosa disappear; these need to be tackled to prevent disordered eating patterns from reappearing.
- There is a close interrelationship between thoughts, mood and behaviour. If one becomes disturbed, a vicious negative circle can then ensue.
- Automatic thoughts are those that just pop into the mind without being consciously formulated. Everyone has them, but they become detrimental when they are repeatedly of a negative nature.
- Cognitive therapy involves recognising and altering negative automatic thoughts.

HOMEWORK ASSIGNMENT FOR STEP 3

- Continue completing your food diary as out-lined in Step 2.
- Remember to continue trying to work towards the 'principles of healthy eating'.
- Using the diaries set out here, try to write down some negative automatic thoughts during the coming week. Put the date in the first column and fill in the other three columns headed 'Emotions', 'Situation' and 'Automatic Thoughts', describing how you felt, what the situation was at the time, and what thoughts came into your head.
- If you find it difficult to identify your automatic thoughts, don't worry; it is a difficult technique to master. Imagine yourself in some situations and think how you would react in each one. For example, ask yourself:
  - What went through your mind when you first looked at this self-help manual?
  - What do you think when you look in the mirror? (Or, if you avoid doing this, what thoughts stop you from doing so?)
  - What goes through your mind when you first meet a new group of people?
- This may get you into the swing of catching the thoughts that just pop into your mind.

Reflections from Step 3

- What have I learned?

_____

_____

_____

_____

_____

_____

- How can I put what I have learned into practice?

_____

_____

_____

_____

_____

_____

_____

- What can I do differently as a result of reading this chapter?

_____

_____

_____

_____

_____

_____

_____

Step 4

Challenging the way you think (II): unhelpful thinking styles

In Step 3 we saw how easy it is to slip into repetitive patterns of thinking that are all too often negative and based on interpretations rather than fact. These negative automatic thoughts can be categorised into various types of *unhelpful thinking styles*. The table below lists the most common types, with a description and example of each.

Table: Unhelpful thinking styles

Type of thinking style	Description of thinking style	Example of thinking style
All or nothing	Seeing things as black or white – no shades of grey.	I failed my driving test. I am a terrible driver. I will just give up.
Over-generalisation	One unfortunate event leads to the assumption that this will happen every time.	Every time I eat a biscuit, I just know I'll binge.
Mental filter	Picking out and dwelling exclusively on the negative/worrying details.	Today was a disaster. I had beaten my calorie allowance by lunchtime.
Disqualifying the positive	Positive experiences don't count for anything. Successes are seen as flukes. No pleasure taken from positive events.	My friend only phoned because they feel sorry for me.
Jumping to conclusions	Assuming the worst even when there is no reason to; expecting failure before trying.	He didn't speak to me because he could see how fat I was.

Catastrophising	Exaggerating your own imperfections. Common misfortunes become disasters.	I made a mistake; how awful. I can never show myself here again. I will never recover.
Emotional reasoning	Taking feelings as facts (e.g. feeling afraid, therefore there must really be some danger).	I feel fat; therefore, I am fat.
'Should', 'must' and 'ought' statements	Thinking you should always be capable of staying calm and never getting angry etc. These statements are over-demanding, unreasonable, and cause unnecessary pressure.	I should be at my goal weight; therefore, I must diet. I ought to be a better daughter.
Labelling/ mislabelling	Labelling yourself on the basis of one mistake. Attribute things going wrong to oneself.	I got that wrong, I'm a useless person. My parents fight because I am an awful daughter.

Table: Diary 3: Challenging thinking errors

Date	Emotions	Situation	Automatic Thoughts	Thinking Errors
12.05.17	Disgust. Anger at myself.	Sitting alone in my room after a binge.	I must not not eat anything tomorrow, to make up for the binge I had tonight.	All or nothing.
14.05.17	Fear. Panic.	Sitting in the dining room at lunchtime.	People are staring at me because they know I am ill.	Jumping to conclusions.
15.05.17	Ashamed. Miserable.	In a department store trying on a dress.	If I can't fit a size ten, I must be overweight. I look so fat in this dress, I may as well go home.	Catastrophising. All or nothing.

If we look again at the excerpt from the cognitive therapy diary of the student mentioned in the last Step, we can now add an extra column to the table to identify the unhelpful thinking styles involved.

With the help of this example, now look back over any negative automatic thoughts that you have recorded and try to decide if these contain any of the types of thinking errors listed in the table. Write down beside the negative automatic thought which thinking error it contains. Sometimes a thought will fit into more than one category, so don't worry if you can't find just one slot for each of your thoughts. There is no right or wrong answer here. You will probably find that there are certain patterns of unhelpful thinking styles that you fall into; in other words, you will have your individual repertoire of habitual unhelpful thinking styles.

Do not try to think of rational responses to your thinking until you have learned to identify the type of unhelpful thinking style first. This stage is important; in order for rational responses to be effective, it is necessary to understand the negative bias or erroneous thinking that you are trying to challenge.

CHAPTER SUMMARY

- Every negative automatic thought has at least one unhelpful thinking style underlying it.
- There are various forms of unhelpful thinking styles, some of which will be more applicable to you than others.
- Identifying which unhelpful thinking styles frequently occur for you is a necessary first step on the way to replacing negative automatic thoughts with more rational responses.

HOMEWORK ASSIGNMENT FOR STEP 4

- Continue completing your food diary and working towards the 'principles of healthy eating'.
- This week, every time you record a negative automatic thought in your diary, try to identify the type (or types) of unhelpful thinking style it represents.
- Try to become aware of the particular kinds of unhelpful thinking style most common in your own thoughts.

Reflections from Step 4

- What have I learned?

_____

_____

_____

_____

_____

_____

- How can I put what I have learned into practice?

_____

_____

_____

_____

_____

_____

- What can I do differently as a result of reading this chapter?

_____

_____

_____

_____

_____

_____

_____

Step 5

Changing your eating patterns

This step begins with an overview of the effects of Anorexia Nervosa and restriction on metabolism. The nature of Anorexia Nervosa almost *tricks* a person into believing many myths surrounding changes in weight that are not in fact true; for example, you may have a powerful fear that you will gain weight in a completely uncontrolled way if you relax your strict controls to the tiniest degree.

Having set out the information relating to the possible barriers that may prevent you from making changes to your food intake – in particular, how and why normal fluctuations occur in weight, and the ways in which the body responds to starvation and to a resumption of normal eating – a system of food portions is introduced by which you can begin to regulate your food intake in a manner that is controlled but not rigid.

Anorexia Nervosa, food intake and metabolism

Weight fluctuations

In studies that have investigated the normal changes in body weight in healthy individuals, a fluctuation of 1 kg (2.2 lb) between consecutive days is common, and fluctuations of 0.5 kg (1.1 lb) very common. In order to understand the reasons for these variations in body weight during short periods, it is worth considering the various components of the human body that can change in size and thus result in change in weight. These are set out in the table below:

Table: Normal variations in body weight

Component of human body	Tissue type	Daily changes in weight when eating a normal diet	Rate of change in weight when restricting
Structural	Bones, ligaments, cartilages, etc.	None.	No change.
Major energy reserves	Muscle, fat.	None.	Changes occur slowly over several weeks of restricting.
Short-term energy reserves	Glycogen (stored in combination with water) in liver.	Minimal fluctuations of 0.5–1.0 kg are common.	Responsible for initial loss of weight in first few days of restricting.

Although loss of mineral from the bones is a common side-effect of extended malnutrition, the effects of this on body weight are small. The body's glycogen stores are specifically designed to provide energy in the short term, i.e. between meals, and in normal circumstances they last only for a few hours. Only when glycogen stores are almost exhausted does the body start to break down muscle and fat stores to release energy.

Figure 5.1: Effects of eating and not eating on energy stores and body weight

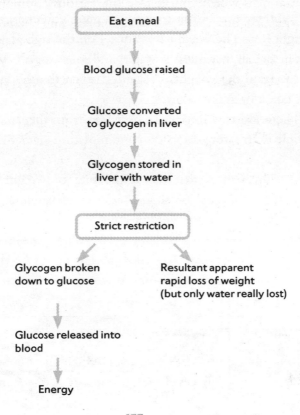

Eat a meal

Blood glucose raised

Glucose converted to glycogen in liver

Glycogen stored in liver with water

Strict restriction

Glycogen broken down to glucose

Resultant apparent rapid loss of weight (but only water really lost)

Glucose released into blood

Energy

Figure 5.1 shows what happens when someone restricts their food intake. When that person starts to eat or to increase their intake, the diagram will flow in the opposite direction. That is, the excess glucose in the blood will be taken up into the liver in combination with water and stored as glycogen. This may occur temporarily following a period of bingeing. This process can also be seen initially when increasing food intake, where there are short-term effects as the body read-justs to receiving the nutrition it has been lacking and needs.

If you look again at the bottom left-hand side of Figure 5.1, you see that burning glycogen gives you energy but no weight loss. The weight loss comes on the right-hand side, but in fact all that is lost is water; and so, as soon as you start to eat again the weight is regained, even though you have not taken in many calories.

There are two important messages from this analysis for people with eating disorders contemplating dietary changes:

- The first is that the initial rate of weight change (whether up or down) in the initial few days of changed eating will not continue.
- The second is that long-term weight **maintenance** does not mean that your weight has to be the same every time you get on the scales.

The body's response to starvation

During the millions of years over which the human body has evolved, it has developed a number of mechanisms to attempt to protect it from adverse environmental circumstances – for example, temperature regulation, responses to lack of oxygen at altitude, etc. Among these adverse environmental circumstances is lack of food, and to protect itself in times of shortage or famine, the body lowers the metabolic rate, enabling itself to survive on less food. This process reinforces the fear of weight gain in people who have rigorously restricted their food intake.

Figure 5.2 shows the changes in the metabolic rate and subsequently in body weight that occur with changes in energy intake. It can be seen that, when a body is starved and there is then an increase in dietary intake to normal, healthy levels/to meet the body's needs, there will be a weight gain in the short term at a greater rate than for a non-starved person, due to the body's protective survival mechanism. This short-term gain can be a difficult time, but after a spell of higher intake the metabolic rate and therefore energy requirements are increased.

There is no evidence of permanently lowered energy requirements in people who increase their intake following starvation. In other words, your body's energy thermostat always resets itself. This means there is no evidence to show initial immediate weight gain as a consequence of lowered metabolic rate/energy intake adjustment persists over time. Evidence has shown us that persisting with the balanced meal plan helps the body to adapt, stabilise and maintain weight gain over time.

These processes of decreasing and increasing metabolic rates apply not just to periods of starvation resulting in

Figure 5.2: Changes in metabolic rate and body weight that occur with changes in energy intake

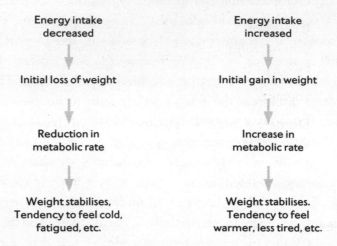

Energy intake decreased	Energy intake increased
↓	↓
Initial loss of weight	Initial gain in weight
↓	↓
Reduction in metabolic rate	Increase in metabolic rate
↓	↓
Weight stabilises, Tendency to feel cold, fatigued, etc.	Weight stabilises. Tendency to feel warmer, less tired, etc.

weight loss, but also to those who starve, binge and purge at a stable weight. The reduction in metabolic rate is reversed when regular eating patterns are re-established; this is particularly helpful if food intake is distributed throughout the day, enabling relearning of normalised eating patterns and providing the body with sustained energy.

Healthy eating

For most people, healthy eating means eating three meals a day and two to three snacks to satisfy hunger. In our clinical experience, we have found that the best way to achieve this balance is to work gradually, day by day, to increase what you are eating to achieve the portions below.

- Try to plan each meal to consist of two courses; for example:

  Breakfast: Cereal with milk followed by toast, and fruit or fruit juice.

  Lunch: Sandwich or wrap, followed by fruit and yoghurt.

  Dinner: Casserole, potatoes with salad/vegetables followed by ice-cream or yoghurt.

It is useful to think of what your food would look like were it to be divided into three equal sections on your plate, as follows:

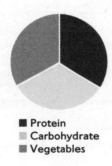

■ Protein
▨ Carbohydrate
▨ Vegetables

Standard measures[1]

- Cooked food: a large serving spoon
- Fluid: 250-ml glass/cup

---

1 Portions sizes courtesy of the Scottish Dieticians' Eating Disorders Clinical Forum.

Examples of carbohydrate portions are as follows:

Table: Examples of carbohydrate portions as described by the Scottish Dieticians' Eating Disorders Clinical Forum

Standard medium cut loaf of bread	2 slices
Dinner-plate-size tortilla wrap	1
Weetabix or shredded wheat	2
Porridge oats uncooked	1 cup measure
Standard bread roll, pitta bread, croissant or bagel	1
Baked potato/sweet potato	One large potato the size of the palm of your hand
Boiled potatoes	3 egg-sized
Cooked pasta or pasta salad or rice	3 heaped serving spoons
Cooked couscous or couscous salad	2 heaped serving spoons
Noodles	1 dried sheet
Oat cakes or crackers	4

Examples of protein portions are as follows:

Table: Examples of protein portions as described by the Scottish Dieticians' Eating Disorders Clinical Forum

Chicken, turkey	1 breast or 3–4 slices of regular packaged slices – not wafer thin
Chilli/bolognaise/curry/casserole	2 serving spoons or 3 if a high vegetable content
Roast meat	3 medium slices
Prawns	10 king prawns or 2 serving spoons of standard prawns
Tuna, salmon, cod etc.	1 steak or fillet
Tinned tuna, salmon	½ large can or 1 small can
Fish fingers	4
Baked beans	½ large can or one small can
Hummus	½ 200 g tub
Cooked beans/lentils	2 serving spoons/½ large cup
Peanuts, cashews, hazel nuts, walnuts etc.	½ cup
Quorn pieces, tofu or soya mince	3 serving spoons
Eggs	2 large eggs
Sausages	2 large thick sausages

Vegetables and salad should not be an excessively large portion and should not take up more than a third of the space on your plate, as illustrated above.

Dairy products are particularly important to include each day as part of your body's recovery, such as milk because it is a mineral-rich food.

Aim to include two portions from the table below (in addition to the protein and carbohydrate portions listed above).

Table: Examples of dairy product portions as described by the Scottish Dieticians' Eating Disorders Clinical Forum

Cheddar etc.	2 matchbox-sized blocks
Cream cheese, e.g. Philadelphia	⅓ of a standard-sized tub
Milk	250-ml cup/glass
Yoghurt	1 standard pot

Snacks are an important part of a healthy eating pattern.

Choose two to three snacks each day from the table opposite.

Table: Examples of snack portions as described by the Scottish Dieticians' Eating Disorders Clinical Forum

The serving size stated equals one portion	
Individual bar of chocolate, e.g. Dairy Milk, Mars, Snickers, Bounty, Twix, etc.	1
Ice-cream on a stick, e.g. Magnum, Feast, Häagen-Dazs, etc.	1
American-style muffin (as sold in coffee shops)	1
Fruit scone or toasted teacake with 1 teaspoon butter/cream and 1 teaspoon jam	1
Scotch pancakes/crumpets with 1 teaspoon butter/cream and 1 teaspoon jam	2
Cereal bars	1
Crisps – standard bag	1
Dried fruit	1 spoon
Nuts, seeds and dried-fruit mix	1 snack pack
Doughnut, Danish pastry, chocolate brownie, etc.	1
Large cookie or chocolate biscuit	1
Plain biscuits, e.g. Digestives or Hobnobs	2
Fruit smoothie	1 cup

Fats and oils

Fat is an essential nutrient. Some of the reasons we need to include fat are as follows:

- It contributes to the structure of hormones, e.g. oestrogen.
- Essential fatty acids are needed for the renewal of cells.
- Fats help prevent heart disease and contribute to the healthy functioning of our brain.

Aim to use one to two portions of fats or oils at each mealtime:

Table: Examples of fats portions as described by the Scottish Dieticians' Eating Disorders Clinical Forum

The serving size stated equals one portion	
Butter, margarine	1 rounded teaspoon
Vegetable oil, olive oil	2 teaspoons
Mayonnaise	2 rounded teaspoons
Salad dressing	4 teaspoons
Crème fraîche	2 rounded teaspoons
Single cream or 'sour' cream	1 serving spoon

Fluids are essential for your health and most people will need six to eight glasses/cups of fluid spread throughout the day, and extra in hotter weather. You can achieve this by including a drink with your meal or snack. Under- and over-consumption of fluid are both problematic, and each can lead to abnormalities in blood. Drinking very little can cause dehydration and symptoms such as headaches and irritability. Over-consuming fluid affects appetite and is used to dampen down the hunger sensation. Therefore, when working towards healthy nutritional intake it is important to check if you are drinking too much or too little. Drinks like water, milk, fruit juices, smoothies or diluted squash count as fluid. Tea and coffee can count towards fluid intake, but drink caffeinated drinks in moderation.

CHAPTER SUMMARY

- It is normal for fluctuations in weight to occur daily.
- Establishing a healthy eating pattern allows the body to hold some energy in reserve in the liver in the form of glycogen.
- Water held with this store of glycogen causes an initial rise in weight when food intake increases, but this will rapidly stabilise.
- Water released from glycogen and excreted in the urine causes an initial weight loss when you starve for a day. This weight loss is not due to loss of muscle or fat.

- Starvation, even as part of a starve/binge/vomit cycle at a stable weight, leads to a decrease in metabolic rate.
- The reverse happens when a normal healthy eating pattern is resumed – that is, metabolic rate increases again. However, a lag in the rise in metabolic rate results in a further initial weight gain, but again this rapidly stabilises.

HOMEWORK ASSIGNMENT FOR STEP 5

- Continue completing your food diary and working towards the 'principles of normal eating'.
- Have a go at implementing the portion system. You will see that there is space in the diary sheets set out in Step 2 to record how many portions you are eating in the first right-hand column headed 'Portion').
- It is a good idea to attempt all the exercises suggested so far before moving on. If you have been unable to do this, don't worry; just go back and try again. There is no limit on how long you can stay with one step.
- Remember that no stage in getting back to a normal eating pattern is easy to accomplish. Don't expect miracles from yourself, and don't forget to reward yourself for any achievements you have made, no matter how small.
- When you feel ready to move on, continue with the next treatment section.

Reflections from Step 5

- What have I learned?

_____

_____

_____

_____

_____

_____

_____

- How can I put what I have learned into practice?

_____

_____

_____

_____

_____

_____

_____

- What can I do differently as a result of reading this chapter?

_____

_____

_____

_____

_____

_____

_____

Step 6

Improving your body image

Anorexia Nervosa and body-image distortion

'Body image' refers to the mental picture that a person has of their own body. It is therefore based on *how one feels about* one's own body, and not on its actual physical appearance. People with Anorexia Nervosa tend to have a very negative body image. Look at Figure 6.1. Do you recognise any of the statements in the figure?

Figure 6.1: Body-image distortion in Anorexia Nervosa

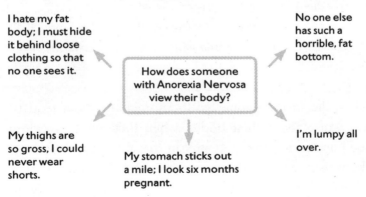

I hate my fat body; I must hide it behind loose clothing so that no one sees it.

No one else has such a horrible, fat bottom.

How does someone with Anorexia Nervosa view their body?

My thighs are so gross, I could never wear shorts.

My stomach sticks out a mile; I look six months pregnant.

I'm lumpy all over.

It is not unusual to mistake strong feelings for facts (e.g. 'I feel lumpy all over, therefore I must be lumpy all over'). This is, however, a thinking error (emotional reasoning). These feelings can become so strong that the person becomes convinced that their body actually looks as bad as it feels. The result is body-image distortion, one of the most distressing features of Anorexia Nervosa.

> *Julie, a twenty-five-year-old student, had suffered from Anorexia Nervosa for two years. When she initially came for help with her eating disorder she had a very distorted body image. Despite being within the normal weight range for someone of her age and height, she was convinced that she looked 'pudgy' all over and that her thighs and buttocks were out of proportion to the rest of her body. As she described herself, 'I just wobble like a jelly.' She could not try on clothes in shops because she felt so ashamed about how she looked and hated places that had numerous mirrors. Whenever she felt down, she dwelt on how fat she was, and whenever she was anxious, e.g. before a job interview, she would get very unhappy and all she could focus on was how awful she looked.*

Like Julie, many people with Anorexia Nervosa tend to feel worse about their bodies when they are feeling low and hopeless in general. It appears that any negative feelings about themselves can be very readily displaced into feelings of fatness. These negative feelings can be the result of all sorts of things. This is especially clear for Julie before her job interviews. In this instance she may well be displacing other negative thoughts, such as anxiety about the interview going badly, on to her body.

Misplacing feelings about yourself on to your body sets up a potential problem: losing weight and trying to change your body shape does not really solve anything, as the underlying issues remain unchanged.

As can be seen from Figure 6.2, body-image dissatisfaction can begin when someone focuses solely on the negative aspects of their body and disregards any positive features. It can arise from dissatisfaction with the whole body or with part of the body; in the latter case that dissatisfaction is then generalised over time. The way someone feels about their body is often reflected in how they view themselves as a person. The last stage of Figure 6.2 shows that having a negative or distorted body image may seriously undermine an individual's self-confidence.

Figure 6.2: Interaction of thinking error and
body-image distortion

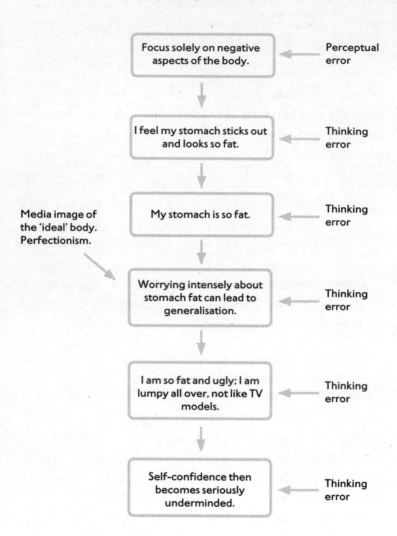

Ideal and reality

Perfectionism can result in a negative body image. The media provide us with an image of the female, in particular, that is portrayed as the 'ideal body'. This image itself is often a distortion: photographs of models are frequently elongated to make the model look taller and thinner than she really is. Therefore, very few people can even approach this ideal body shape. Indeed, some ideas of beauty stress the rarity value of 'beauty', and what is considered beautiful or ideal in any particular culture is nearly always unachievable by the generality of the population, e.g. small feet in China, plumpness in some Third World countries, thinness in Western society. However, people who feel that they have to achieve perfection in all aspects of their life can quickly become obsessed with the fact that their body is not how they want it to be, and this leads to distortion of their own image and further distress as they strive to reach an unattainable goal.

If you avoid looking at and touching your body, and recognising it as it is, this can perpetuate negative feelings about it, possibly to the extent that you become *phobic* about your body, or parts of it. As with all phobias, the best way of overcoming this is to reduce avoidance behaviour and confront the fear. The more you avoid the subject of the phobia, the stronger the phobia becomes. Therefore, the rest of this step sets out some suggestions for ways you can come to accept and appreciate your body more. Like all the other stages in this programme, they will take perseverance and practice.

While you are carrying out these activities, use the cognitive techniques you have learned to challenge thoughts about your body.

Writing your body's history

Understanding where your negative body image or even body hatred comes from may help you gradually change it. One way of doing this is to write a history of your body and the way you view this.

- It is probably easiest to do this by taking particular points in time; say, at age five, age eight, age eleven and age fifteen.

- It is sometimes useful to get out old family photos and use those as triggers to the way you were feeling at the time.

- Sometimes it may be a particular family event or scene, which hasn't been captured in a family photo but which you can remember clearly. Try to think back to a time when you felt comfortable about your body and start there.

- If you are looking at a family photo, ask yourself where you are standing in relation to other family members? Do you look happy or sad? Do you look part of the group, or are you alone? Is the family including or excluding you? What was going on in the family at this time? How were you feeling about yourself and your body?

- Do this for each page and write a story about how your negative body image developed.
- Don't stop at the point at which your Anorexia Nervosa developed. If there are photos after that, include these and ask yourself the same questions.

Learning to accept or even like your body again is not going to be easy. It is going to take a lot of time and a lot of repetition of small simple tasks. Here are some things that may help.

Re-writing the story. Re-write your story as though you hadn't developed a negative body image. What would have been different? Would you have been more effective at changing things within the family? Would relationships have worked out differently? This may be hard to do, and it may feel unbelievable, but try and persevere. Anything which puts different ideas, alternatives, in your mind may help.

Create an alternative body image (schema). Make this a kind, warm, benevolent compassionate 'you'. One that is not critical of you, not judgemental, less perfectionist. Take this other 'you' around with you. Imagine it sitting on your shoulder or standing behind you. When you have negative body experiences, listen to what it has to say about you and the way you are.

Be media savvy. Not all people with Anorexia Nervosa develop their problem because of media images or media pressure, but some do. Remember that we live in a very distorted world. Images that you see on social media, in magazines and on TV are frequently unreal. They are photographed in certain ways with particular lighting; they are often air-brushed and sometimes vertically distorted. Repeatedly say to yourself when you see these images: this is not reality; this is a distortion.

Keep a positive diary. Your body image has been maintained by thousands of occasions when you have said to yourself something critical about your body or negatively compared yourself with others. Anorexia Nervosa causes you to focus on these negative aspects and miss out the positive ones. Try and experiment for a week, only noting down positive or pleasurable experiences you have in relation to your body and ignoring the negative ones. This will help you correct the bias that is built into your thinking.

Body-image activities

The following suggested activities may help you to think more about your body–image distortion, and to focus on why this may have come about. For each exercise, set aside some time when you know that you will not be required to do anything else and will have peace and quiet. You may find it helps to work through each one on paper. It is a good idea to use a notebook – it could be the same one in which you keep your food diaries, or a different one – to record your thoughts and feelings as you work through these exercises; you will then have the notes readily to hand and can refer back to them when you want to in the future.

SEVEN ACTIVITIES TO HELP YOU TO THINK ABOUT YOUR BODY-IMAGE DISTORTION

1. Try to imagine yourself in ten or twenty years' time. Where are you and what are you doing? What are your aims and ambitions? Ask yourself if you are on track for achieving these goals, or if you need to make changes. Write your goals down and look at them when you are low and in need of a focus.

2. Look at who you are now. Ask yourself how you see yourself and write this down. Then ask yourself how you think you are seen by others and write this down. Compare the two. What are the differences and what are the similarities? Turn over on to a new page. Consider how you would like to see yourself, and how you would like to be seen by others. Write both down. What would need to be changed in order for you to be seen as you would like, both by yourself and by others? How would you go about making such change or changes?

3. Think of some woman who impresses you yet is not excessively thin. It may be a relative, a friend, an actress, a sportswoman, a business-woman . . . What is it that impresses you – that makes you notice and respect her? It could, for example, be style, posture, confidence,

energy, vivaciousness, intelligence, sense of control and purpose, or any one or more of a number of things. Ask yourself if you have any of these qualities; if not, think what you could do to cultivate them. Do you think weight and shape are of such importance to the person you respect? If not, what do you think is likely to be important to her?

4. Stand in front of a mirror and look at your body. For each negative statement you come up with about your reflection, make yourself say something positive – even if you do not believe it yet. Write these positive affirmations down and practise repeating them when you find yourself criticising your body. Though this will feel quite forced to start with, try to persevere.

5. Does your body image restrict you in any way? Are there some things you avoid doing? Examples may be looking in a full-length mirror, wearing a bikini on holiday, trying on clothes in a communal changing room, using communal showers, etc. Write a list of these and make a resolution to try to confront rather than avoid these uncomfortable situations. Try to do these things and see if you can think differently.

6. Pamper yourself physically. Though you may be in a pattern of being critical about yourself,

take time to look after what you do have. Treat yourself to a long, luxurious, hot bath and afterwards spend time massaging aromatic oils into your skin from head to toe. Take time to linger on each part of your anatomy and try to counterbalance each negative thought with a positive one. If you think, 'My thighs are so fat and flabby', set against this, 'My skin feels so soft and smooth.'

7. Let's talk exercise. Do you do exercise for pleasure or out of guilt and anxiety? What is exercise *for*? For your pleasure, enjoyment and fulfilment? Or to burn calories and fat and make you thinner? I suggest it may be the latter. If so, try to think of something you would actively *enjoy* doing: if you really do want to be physically active, perhaps a dance class, or aqua-aerobics; or it could be something less strenuous, such as seeing films, visiting art galleries, reading novels. The important thing is to allocate time for activities you genuinely *enjoy*. If it helps, write down a selection of possibilities and score them on a scale of 1–10 for enjoyment. Make the effort to give highest priority to the ones you think will give you most enjoyment.

Breaking the cycle

As you try to break the cycle of body-image distortion and renewed urges to eat less and get thinner, ask yourself the following questions. They may help you to be more aware of the patterns of thought that have become habitual to you, and of *why* you think the way you do, and so help you to begin to break the automatic connection between perceived/distorted body image and self-esteem that reinforces the symptoms of Anorexia Nervosa.

- Try to identify the times when you feel worst about your body. Are you in fact misplacing other problems on to your body? What might these underlying issues be? Boredom? Anxiety? Anger? Try to identify what is really troubling you.
- Many people have described the onset of their dieting as being associated with a feeling of being 'out of control' of some aspect to their life. Dieting to them felt like something that they could control, and this was a relief at the time. Is there anything in your life that feels out of your control, and is increasing the urge to control your body weight by way of compensating for this?
- Is your body-image distortion making the problem worse?
- Are you seeing only the negative aspects of your shape and forgetting the rest of your body?
- Could you see your body more positively? Try not to focus on body parts that you are dissatisfied with. See your body as a whole.

The key point is to try to break the connection between how you view yourself as a person and how you visualise *your body*.

CHAPTER SUMMARY

- People who suffer from Anorexia Nervosa tend to have a very negative body image, i.e. they feel that parts of themselves are much fatter and uglier than they really are, and they translate this feeling into a belief that they are fat and ugly.

- A person with Anorexia Nervosa often has a view of themselves as a person who is strongly influenced, if not dominated, by feelings about their body, which severely undermines self-confidence.

- Perfectionism can lead to a negative body image and much misery while striving for the unobtainable goal of the 'perfect' body.

- For someone suffering from Anorexia Nervosa, general negative feelings, e.g. feelings of hopelessness or depression, can readily be displaced into feelings of fatness.

- Avoiding looking at or touching your body perpetuates negative thoughts and feelings about it.

HOMEWORK ASSIGNMENT FOR STEP 6

- Continue with your diary as before.
- Look back through the diaries you have amassed over the past few weeks, and ask yourself the following questions:
    - What connections are there between eating and feelings?
    - What are your automatic thoughts about weight, shape and food?
    - Do the same thoughts tend to keep cropping up?
    - Are you able to challenge any of these thoughts?
    - If you are able to challenge them, does it make any difference to your *behaviour*?
    - Which of the various coping strategies presented in the manual so far are you finding helpful to you?
- Try to work through all the activities 1–7 on body image listed above and write your body history. This may be quite draining for you but do try to persevere; they may well give you a lot of useful information.
- If you have been unable to carry out these exercises so far, don't worry; go back and read through them again, and have another go.
- When you feel ready, continue with the next treatment section.

Reflections from Step 6

- What have I learned?

_____

_____

_____

_____

_____

_____

- How can I put what I have learned into practice?

_____

_____

_____

_____

_____

_____

- What can I do differently as a result of reading this chapter?

_____

_____

_____

_____

_____

_____

Step 7

Developing assertiveness

For someone with Anorexia Nervosa, the rationale behind learning to be more assertive is that it may provide you with a tool other than food avoidance. Learning to be assertive requires practice, and it is not easy to teach by way of a self-help manual. However, the information presented here can be used as a set of guidelines with which you can experiment, to give you a starting point on which you can build as you gain in confidence.

What is assertiveness?

What does 'being assertive' mean? To start with, it may be useful to review a 'Bill of Assertiveness Rights', taken from Manuel J. Smith's book *When I Say No, I Feel Guilty*:

1. You have the right to judge your own behaviour, thoughts and emotions and to take the responsibility for their initiation and consequences upon yourself.

2. You have the right to offer no reasons or excuses for justifying your behaviour.
3. You have the right to judge if you are responsible for finding solutions to other people's problems.
4. You have the right to change your mind.
5. You have the right to make mistakes – and be responsible for them.
6. You have the right to say, 'I don't know.'
7. You have the right to be independent of the goodwill of others before coping with them.
8. You have the right to be 'illogical' in making decisions.
9. You have the right to say, 'I don't understand.'
10. You have the right to say, 'I don't care.'

In any form of communication, be it verbal or non-verbal, there are three different ways to act:

1. Assertively.
2. Aggressively.
3. Non-assertively.

So, what differentiates these three different types of behaviour?

Assertion

As you can see from Figure 7.1, assertive behaviour involves standing up for your own rights – expressing your thoughts, feelings and beliefs in a way that:

- is direct, honest and appropriate, and
- does not violate the rights of another person.

It involves respect, not submission. You are respecting your own needs and rights, as well as accepting that the other person also has needs and rights.

Figure 7.1: Assertive, aggressive and non-assertive behaviour

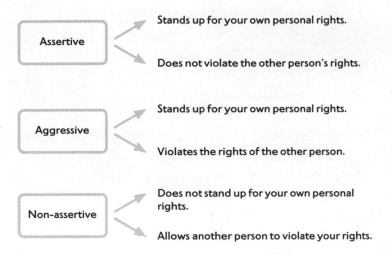

Assertive → Stands up for your own personal rights.
→ Does not violate the other person's rights.

Aggressive → Stands up for your own personal rights.
→ Violates the rights of the other person.

Non-assertive → Does not stand up for your own personal rights.
→ Allows another person to violate your rights.

Aggression

This involves standing up for personal rights and expressing your own thoughts, feelings and beliefs in a way that:

- is usually inappropriate, and
- always violates the rights of the other person.

The usual goal of aggression is domination and winning, forcing the other person to lose. Winning is ensured by humiliating or overpowering other people so that they become weaker and less able to express and defend their needs and rights. The message is:

- This is what I think – you're stupid for believing differently.
- This is what I want – what you want isn't important.
- This is what I feel – your feelings don't count.

Non-assertion

This involves not standing up for your own rights by:

- not expressing honest feelings, thoughts and beliefs, and thereby
- letting others violate your personal rights.

The message communicated is:

- I don't count – you can take advantage of me.
- My feelings don't matter – only yours do.
- I'm nothing – you're superior.

So, it means you are not respecting your own rights and needs. The goal of non-assertion is to appease others and avoid conflict at any cost.

Different responses in the same scenario

Figure 7.2 shows three different possible responses to a single scenario: one aggressive, one assertive, one non–assertive. The following exercise will help to clarify what we mean by the words 'assertive', 'non-assertive' and 'aggressive', consolidate the different types of responses available to you and help you to see which type you routinely use.

Figure 7.2: Assertive, aggressive and non-assertive responses

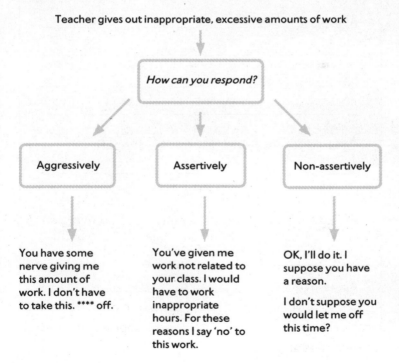

Teacher gives out inappropriate, excessive amounts of work

How can you respond?

| Aggressively | Assertively | Non-assertively |

You have some nerve giving me this amount of work. I don't have to take this. **** off.

You've given me work not related to your class. I would have to work inappropriate hours. For these reasons I say 'no' to this work.

OK, I'll do it. I suppose you have a reason.

I don't suppose you would let me off this time?

For each situation below, make suggestions for what you think the three types of responses might be: i.e. not how you would behave under the circumstances, but how you think an aggressive, non-assertive or assertive person might respond.

(a) You are out for a works night out in mixed company. During a friendly difference of opinion one of the men says quite seriously, '*Of course women are definitely the inferior race. It's been proved.*'

Aggressive: _____

_____

Non-assertive: _____

_____

Assertive: _____

_____

(b) You are with friends deciding which movie you are all going to see. Someone suggests a movie that you have already seen and didn't like at all.

Aggressive: _____

_____

Non-assertive: _____

_____

Assertive: _____

_____

(c) A colleague from work criticises another mutual colleague. You feel the criticism is unjustified.

Aggressive: _____

_____

Non-assertive: _____

_____

Assertive: _____

_____

(d) You bought an expensive designer dress that you really liked. After the first wash the stitching around the left shoulder seam started to come undone.

Aggressive: _____

_____

Non-assertive: _____

_____

Assertive: _____

_____

(e) You return a pair of trousers because the stitching is faulty. It was the only pair of trousers in that style that were your size. The assistant offers you an exchange or a credit note.

Aggressive: _____

_____

Non-assertive: _____

_____

Assertive: _____

_____

(f) You have whizzed home during your lunch break and are quickly eating a bowl of soup before rushing back to work. The doorbell rings and a smartly dressed man, saying that he is from the gas company, asks to be let in to check your piping as part of a safety campaign. You have had no warning of this and are in a hurry to get back to work.

Aggressive: _____

_____

Non-assertive: _____

_____

Assertive: _____

_____

(g) You have gone to a newly opened restaurant for lunch. They are very slow to take your order, and when your food arrives, it is cold.

Aggressive: _____

_____

Non-assertive: _____

_____

Assertive: _____

_____

Now look back over your answers and note, for each case, the following points.

Reasons for acting assertively

- *Why be assertive rather than non-assertive?* Non-assertive people often fear losing the respect of others. However, non-assertion does not guarantee approval.

- *Why be assertive rather than aggressive?* Aggression does not guarantee successful control over other people. It just means they will probably go 'underground' with their feelings. Assertive behaviour may help to increase your feelings of 'self-control' and makes you feel more confident.

- Aggression will probably make you feel more vulnerable. Assertion rather than aggression results in closer relationships with others. You won't necessarily win, but both parties can at least partially achieve some goals and get their needs met.

Assertive behaviour increases your own self-respect, leading to greater self-confidence and thus reducing the need for others' approval. Usually, people respect and admire those who are responsibly assertive, showing respect for self and others. Assertion results in individuals having their needs satisfied and preferences respected.

Types of assertion

Now that we can differentiate assertive behaviour from aggressive and non-assertive, we need to look to different types of assertion and when to use them.

Figure 7.3 shows five different types of assertion, each of which suits a different situation. We will look at each one in greater depth and give examples to show the type of situation in which it is used most appropriately.

Figure 7.3: The five types of assertion

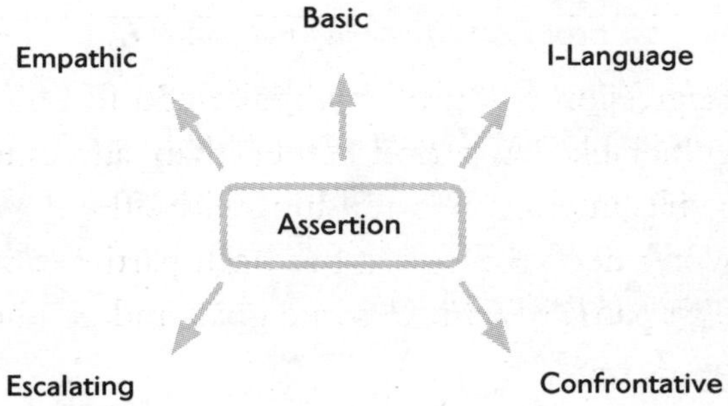

Basic assertion

This is expressing basic personal rights, beliefs or feelings; e.g.

- When being asked an important question for which you are unprepared: '*I'd like to have a few minutes to think that over.*'
- When it is apparent you don't need advice: '*I don't want any more advice.*'
- Also, expressing affection and appreciation to others: '*I like you.*' '*I care for you a lot.*' '*You're someone special to me.*'

Empathic assertion

This is expressing your needs/feelings, but also showing sensitivity to the other person; e.g.

- When two people are chatting loudly while a meeting is in progress: '*You may not realise it, but your talking is starting to make it hard for me to hear what's going on in the meeting. Would you keep it down?*'
- When having some furniture delivered: '*I know it's hard to say when the truck will come, but I would like an estimate of the arrival time.*'

Escalating assertion

This starts with a minimal assertive response, usually achieving the goal with a minimum of effort. When the other person fails to respond and continues to violate your rights, you gradually increase the assertion and become increasingly firm without becoming aggressive. For example, say you are in a bar with a friend and a man repeatedly offers to buy you drinks.

- Your first response is: '*That's very nice of you to offer, but we're here to catch up on some news. Thanks anyway.*'
- Next time you say: '*No thank you. We really would rather talk to each other.*'
- Finally, you say: '*This is the third and last time I am going to tell you we don't want your company. Please leave.*'

The final, blunt refusal was appropriate because the earlier assertions were ignored.

Confrontative assertion

This is used when the other person's words contradict what he/she does. This type of assertion involves describing what the other person said would be done, what they actually did, and what you want done; e.g.

- *'I said it was OK to borrow my phone charger as long as you checked with me first. Now you're borrowing it without asking. I'd like to know why you did that.'*

I-Language assertion

This is assertively expressing difficult negative feelings; e.g.

- *'When your half of the desk is so messy, I start feeling angry and that upsets me. I'd like you to be neater and more organised.'*
- *'When I'm constantly interrupted, I lose my train of thought and begin to feel that my ideas are not important to me. I start feeling hurt and angry. I'd like you to make a point of waiting until I've finished speaking.'*

Use of assertion

If behaving assertively is new to you, you might find it

helpful to use Figure 7.4 to formulate a basic plan of how you are going to approach each new situation.

If, to begin with, you don't feel confident enough to behave assertively with everyone, then try doing some role-playing with a close friend at home before launching the new, assertive you on the rest of the world.

Figure 7.4: An approach to behaving assertively

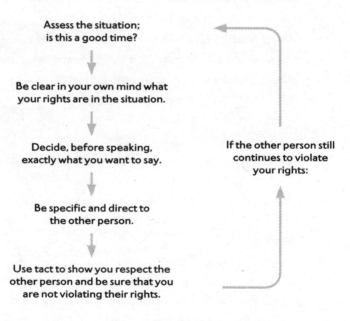

Assess the situation; is this a good time?

Be clear in your own mind what your rights are in the situation.

Decide, before speaking, exactly what you want to say.

Be specific and direct to the other person.

Use tact to show you respect the other person and be sure that you are not violating their rights.

If the other person still continues to violate your rights:

Beccie, a twenty-seven-year-old office worker, had suffered from Anorexia Nervosa for five years. She had low self-esteem and was very miserable both at home and at work. After a hard day at work she came home to start the cooking, cleaning and ironing. The list of tasks was endless. She was unable to see any way out, feeling that it was her duty to do all this work and feeling guilty for moaning about it. Occasionally she felt like screaming at her husband for help, but she was scared of what he might do in response.

A friend suggested that Beccie join an assertiveness class with her. She decided to go along although she was doubtful that it would help. She was taught about 'The Bill of Assertiveness Rights' and how to act assertively, practising in class by role-playing. Soon she began to realise that looking after the home was not her sole responsibility and that it was acceptable to ask her family for help. Her family put up some resistance initially as they did not like having to do 'extra' work, but she prodded them along, using her new-found assertive techniques. Soon Beccie found that life was somewhat easier and more enjoyable.

Why don't people act assertively?

Reasons why people act non-assertively

Like Beccie in the case history described above, you may have more than one reason why you don't act assertively. In her case it was a combination of failure to accept that she had personal rights, and anxiety about the negative consequences. Once she became convinced that she did have rights and feelings, that she was entitled to just as much consideration as any other human being, she was able to act more assertively, at which point she found that the negative consequences were not as bad as she had feared.

Other reasons for acting non-assertively are:

- Mistaking firm assertion for aggression.
- Mistaking non-assertion for politeness . . . but is it polite, or is it actually dishonest?
- Mistaking non-assertion for being helpful, when really it is exactly the opposite!
- Poor social skills. This is where role-playing can be particularly helpful, allowing you to practise assertion in safe surroundings.

If you are frequently non-assertive, you will feel a growing loss of self-esteem, and an increasing sense of hurt and anger. Internal tension may result (as with Beccie). Close relationships can be difficult without honest expression of thoughts and feelings.

Reasons why people act aggressively

- Out of powerlessness and a feeling of being under threat.
- As an extreme counter-reaction to previous non-assertion.

- In over-reaction due to past emotional experiences.
- Because of mistaken beliefs about aggression, i.e. that this is the only way to get through.
- Through not knowing how to be assertive.

If you are frequently aggressive, you might lose or fail to establish close relationships and feel that you have to be constantly on the watch for counter-attacks. You might lose your job, miss out on promotion, develop high blood pressure, and feel misunderstood and unloved; and you may feel guilt, shame or embarrassment after your aggression.

CHAPTER SUMMARY

- Assertion involves standing up for your own personal rights while not violating those of others.
- Non-assertion allows others to violate your personal rights and may lead to them losing respect and pitying you.
- Aggression violates the rights of others and does not guarantee successful control over them.
- Assertive behaviour increases your own self-respect, leading to greater self-confidence and thus reducing the need for others' approval.

- There are several types of assertion; to maximise the impact of any of them it is important to use timing and tact.
- Role-playing is a good way of increasing your confidence in using assertive behaviour before trying it out in the 'real' world.

HOMEWORK ASSIGNMENT FOR STEP 7

- Continue your diary as before.
- Review last week's diary. Identify situations in which you are not assertive. Write them down. In what way are you not assertive in each situation? How could you be more assertive in each situation?
- Practise being more assertive in the situations you have identified as being problematic. Record the results of your more assertive behaviour and compare them with when you are less assertive. How does it feel to be more assertive?
- Changing your behaviour from aggressive or non-assertive to assertive can be a difficult and slow task. Remember that it has probably taken you years to perfect your present behaviour, so it will take rather more than a day to change it!

- An important first step is to recognise the three types of behaviour and which one you most commonly use. If you have not managed this yet, don't worry; work through the step again at your own pace until you feel comfortable with it.
- When you feel ready, continue with the next treatment section.

Reflections from Step 7

- What have I learned?

_____

_____

_____

_____

_____

_____

_____

• How can I put what I have learned into practice?

_____

_____

_____

_____

_____

_____

• What can I do differently as a result of reading this chapter?

_____

_____

_____

_____

_____

_____

_____

Step 8

Dealing with anxiety

It has been calculated that as many as 70 per cent of women with Anorexia Nervosa also experience some type of anxiety disorder at some point in the illness. Anxiety can have significant effects on your quality of life, as the following example shows.

Megan, a twenty-five-year-old shop assistant, had been living with Anorexia Nervosa for seven years. She hated going out but her friends always nagged her to go and she was afraid she would look 'different' if she refused.

On the days leading up to going out, she would find herself becoming irritable and edgy, worrying excessively about what to wear, what she would say, and what others would think of her. When she was out, she found herself to be sweating profusely and often felt others would hear her heart beating, it was so loud. She was always exhausted and miserable by the time she arrived back home.

Overcoming anxiety involves first understanding the causes and symptoms.

Figure 8.1 shows the many ways in which anxiety and Anorexia Nervosa interact. Are you a stress eater (turning to food for comfort, grazing, etc.) or a stress dieter?

Figure 8.1: Anorexia Nervosa and anxiety

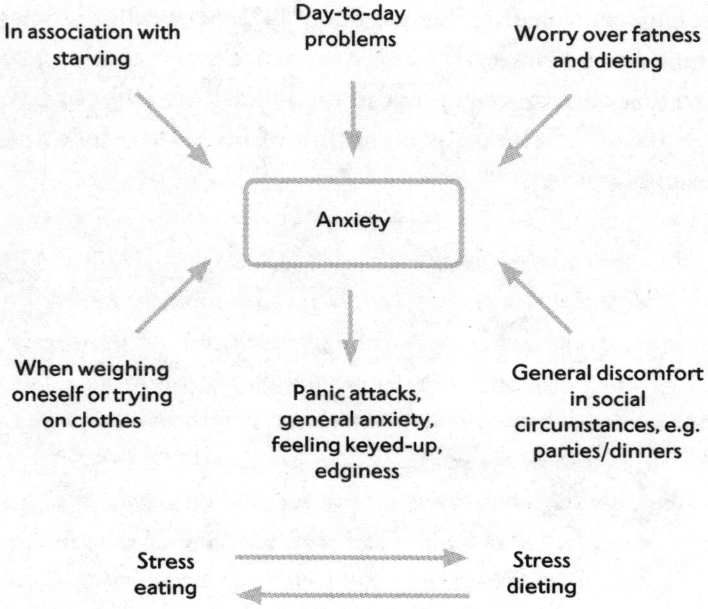

In association with starving

Day-to-day problems

Worry over fatness and dieting

Anxiety

When weighing oneself or trying on clothes

Panic attacks, general anxiety, feeling keyed-up, edginess

General discomfort in social circumstances, e.g. parties/dinners

Stress eating

Stress dieting

Symptoms of anxiety

The effects of anxiety can be felt as physical sensations, as in Megan's case, described above. These physical effects are very real and are determined by the body's automatic response to perceived danger, whereby the body prepares itself for 'fight or flight or freeze' in the face of perceived danger by raising the heart rate, quickening breathing and producing adrenaline. Problems arise when this reaction occurs in a situation that would not normally call for such a dramatic response.

Hyperventilation, or 'over-breathing', can itself produce a range of frightening sensations that may trigger a continuous rise in anxiety and thus further symptoms. For this reason, if you find yourself hyperventilating, it is worth learning how to calm your breathing. Other books in this series deal with the causes and symptoms of anxiety in greater depth and contain useful suggestions on counteracting symptoms: see *Overcoming Anxiety* by Helen Kennerley, *Overcoming Panic* by Derrick Silove and Vijaya Manicavasagar, and *Overcoming Social Anxiety and Shyness* by Gillian Butler.

Anxiety can also produce changes in your thinking, again as we saw with Megan, who found herself to be irritable and edgy before social events. Figure 8.3 shows some of the other effects of anxiety on thinking.

Figure 8.2: The physical effects of anxiety

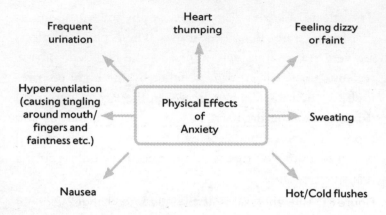

Figure 8.3: Anxiety-induced changes in thinking

Figure 8.4: How anxiety levels change over time

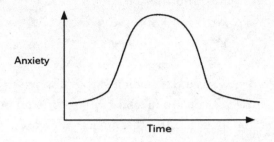

Figure 8.5: How anorexic feelings about food change over time

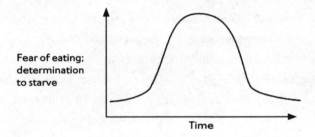

Looking at Figures 8.2 and 8.3 and Megan's case history, think about your own experience of anxiety:

- Note down any symptoms, either mentioned above, or any others that you have experienced, which you think may be attributed to anxiety.
- Have you ever had a panic attack? If so, what physical and psychological symptoms occur for you?

- What does anxiety feel like to you? In your body? In your mind? Emotionally?

Anxiety and eating

Take a look at Figure 8.4, which shows how your level of anxiety changes if you are in, and *stay in*, a stressful situation. The most important point is that anxiety subsides with time. However, if the anxiety-provoking situation is avoided, it becomes quite difficult to believe that the symptoms can decrease; therefore, one of the first steps in learning to deal with anxiety is to acknowledge that there are anxiety symptoms and, once these are acknowledged, to *stay within the situation*, however uncomfortable it seems, in order to discover that the symptoms can be tolerated and will decrease.

Can the same curve apply to feelings about food and eating? Imagine the same graph with a different label on the left-hand axis, as shown in Figure 8.5 – and the answer is clearly 'yes'. Again, it can be difficult to believe that these feelings are tolerable; the easiest option seems to be to 'give in' and avoid eating. But this could in fact be described as *avoiding* the anxiety; and the result is that the anorexic behaviour is reinforced. In order to overcome symptoms of Anorexia Nervosa you may have to learn to cope with the increasing tension by using anxiety-management techniques and finding distractions from eating-related anxiety. It is also important to tackle the negative automatic thoughts that could trigger a binge; refer back to Steps 3 and 4 to remind yourself about how to do this.

Relaxation techniques

Increasing tension can be tackled directly by using relaxation techniques. Relaxation can also be used to develop an awareness of physical tension that may build up to the point where it becomes problematic. To begin with, it may be useful to use one of the many relaxation apps or podcasts that are readily available. These will take you through a sequence of stages, prompting you to relax the main muscle groups of the body in turn and often inviting you to imagine yourself in a safe, relaxing situation, e.g. in a sunny garden or on a private beach. Figure 8.6 sets out some guidelines for using such an app.

Figure 8.6: How to approach a relaxation exercise

1. Set aside twenty minutes per day.

2. Find a quiet room where you won't be disturbed.

3. Lie on a bed, or the floor, or sit on a comfortable chair or mat.

4. Loosen tight clothing – e.g. belts, top, shirt buttons – take off shoes.

5. Start the app when ready; keep to pace (don't be tempted to jump ahead).

To benefit from relaxation training, you need to learn the art by practising it daily.

Remember:

- Concentrate on breathing slowly, smoothly and evenly, and not too deeply, throughout the exercises.
- Practise relaxation only when there is no time pressure – not, for example, fifteen minutes before you are due to leave for work.
- If you can, set aside a regular time each day for your relaxation exercises, e.g. after work, after your evening meal or just before going to bed. Remember, though, that lapses are likely to happen. What is important is to get back into the habit of practising your relaxation, as quickly as possible.

Other suggestions of ways to relax, including how to make your own relaxation recording, are given in Step 10 below, 'Coping strategies for the future'.

CHAPTER SUMMARY

- People who have Anorexia Nervosa very often suffer from symptoms of anxiety.
- Symptoms can be physical – e.g. palpitations, hyperventilation – or emotional – e.g. irritability.

- If you stay in an anxiety–provoking situation, with time the symptoms of anxiety will decrease.
- To overcome the symptoms of Anorexia Nervosa, it may be necessary to learn to cope with increasing tension using relaxation and distraction techniques.

HOMEWORK ASSIGNMENT FOR STEP 8

- Continue your diary as before.
- Remember the 'principles of normal eating'.
- Practise relaxation (if possible using a relaxation recording of some sort – even, perhaps, one you've made yourself), taking care to follow the instructions given in Figure 8.6.
- Learning relaxation techniques can be very worthwhile in helping you to overcome your eating disorder. If you have not managed to practise relaxation regularly so far, then decide right now what time of the day is easiest for you to set aside for relaxation practice and make sure that you use that time solely for that purpose. Spend a few days practising the technique before moving on.
- If you feel that you have managed to grasp the basics of a relaxation technique, then, in your own time, turn over the page to start the next step.

Reflections from Step 8

- What have I learned?

_____

_____

_____

_____

_____

_____

_____

- How can I put what I have learned into practice?

_____

_____

_____

_____

_____

_____

- What can I do differently as a result of reading this chapter?

_____

_____

_____

_____

_____

_____

_____

Step 9

Managing your relationships

Neither you nor your Anorexia Nervosa exists in a vacuum, and it is important to consider how family, friends and work relationships are intertwined in your situation. Interpersonal difficulties may be involved in the development and maintenance of the Anorexia Nervosa and in preventing you from recovering; whether or not your close relationships have anything to do with the development of your eating disorder, they will almost inevitably be markedly affected by the fact that you have Anorexia Nervosa. This step is designed to help you understand your personal relationships and to manage them effectively.

Stage I: An interpersonal network map

Draw a map that includes all your interpersonal relationships. An example is given in Figure 9.1. Think of all the people you interact with and include them in the map: family, friends, those involved in treating you. It need not be limited to humans; include pets if you have them, as they can be significant in your life. Now draw two separate maps, one for before your Anorexia Nervosa began and one for afterwards. Once you have done this, set the maps aside for a day or two and then go back to them again. You may be surprised to find that you have overlooked important relationships that you can now add.

Why draw an interpersonal network map?

1. It helps you to summarise all your relationships on one page.
2. It presents your relationships in picture form.
3. It may help you identify which relationships you would like to try and change.

How to draw an interpersonal network map

1. Make a list of all your important relationships. Think of all your different social settings: home, school or work, and recreation. Include pets if they are important. Include all relationships, distant as well as close – any that are important. Maybe colour-code using different colours for family, work colleagues etc.
2. Begin by putting yourself in the middle of the map.
3. Add each person's name in a circle. The closer the relationship, the closer to you, in the middle, that circle should be.

4. Indicate the intensity of the relationship with multiple lines.

5. Indicate the direction of the relationship with arrows, e.g.

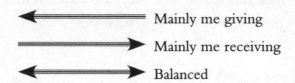

Mainly me giving

Mainly me receiving

Balanced

6. Try out different versions of the map – pick one that feels right for you:

   (a) How I would like my interpersonal world to be.
   (b) How my interpersonal world was before my Anorexia Nervosa.
   (c) How my interpersonal world might be now, without Anorexia Nervosa.
   (d) How my interpersonal world will be in ten years if my Anorexia Nervosa stays the same.

7. Notice the differences and set yourself goals for the relationship you would like to try and alter.

8. Show the maps to those who are important in your life and get their comments.

Figure 9.1: Iman's first map – as she sees it now

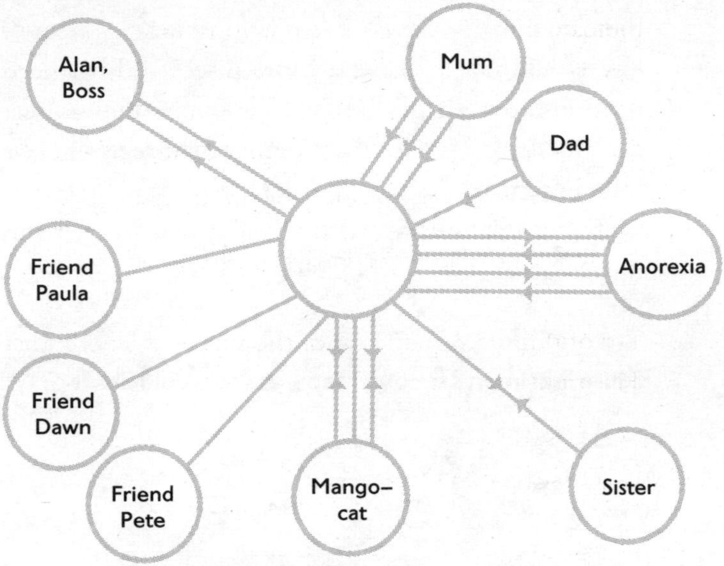

Comments on Iman's maps

In the first map, as things are now:

- Iman has included her Anorexia Nervosa as a relationship.
- Currently it is the most powerful and closest relationship she has.
- She would like to have a more equal and balanced relationship with her mother and father in which both are a bit less involved in her life.
- She has grown apart from her sister and her best friend Paula and would like to repair these relationships.

241

- She spent much time thinking about her relationships with her friends and found she couldn't reliably assess them.
- She would like to have a more direct and balanced relationship with her boss. She supports him a great deal, he demands a lot from her, and she feels she gets little in return.
- Only her relationship with Mango, her cat, remains unchanged.

Figure 9.2: Iman's second map – as she would like it

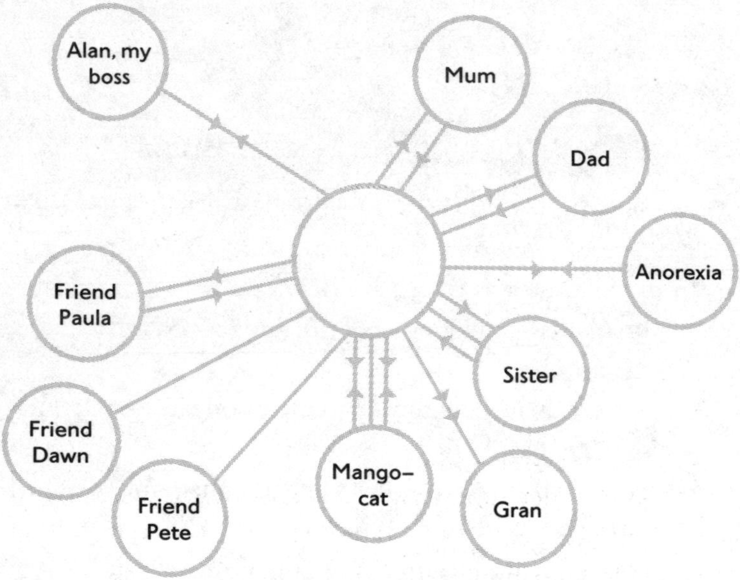

In the second map, as she would like her relationships to be:

- Iman realises that for things to change she will have to separate from her Anorexia Nervosa.
- She remembers her granny, who lives 400 miles away, and how important she used to be to her. She wants to revive that relationship and give back to her granny, who is now old and ill.
- She decides to suspend judgement on her relationships with Dawn and Peter, about whom she still feels confused. She needs to gather more evidence and feedback.
- She decides to confide in her sister, and to try to change that relationship first.

Stage 2: Examining your relationships

Now, working through your relationship map, take each relationship in turn and begin to examine it. Ask yourself questions such as:

- How often do I see this person?
- Who initiates the contact?
- Who decides what we do or what we talk about?
- Who terminates the contact?
- How happy am I with the frequency of contact?

- How happy am I with the quality of this relationship?
- How balanced or mutual does it feel? (Is it a relationship where I feel I give but don't receive, or a relationship where I take and give little?)
- How would I like this relationship to be?
- Do I want to increase the frequency of contact or decrease it?
- Do I want to alter the nature or intensity of contact?
- Am I happy leaving things just as they are?

Obviously, going through each relationship asking all these questions may take quite a time – but it is an exercise that is worth doing.

If you feel stuck, you can ask questions about the whole of your interpersonal network, such as:

- If I suddenly became ill, who would I turn to for help?
- If I wanted to borrow money at very short notice, who would I ask?
- If I wanted to confide in someone, who would I choose?
- If I wanted practical advice, who would I choose?
- If I wanted to have fun, who would I go to?

You should now have a very rich picture of your interpersonal world. If you have done the whole exercise twice, once for the map before you developed Anorexia Nervosa and once for the map with Anorexia Nervosa, you should also have a clearer picture of how your eating disorder has altered and interacts with your relationships.

You should also have some idea of how you would like your interpersonal world to be and how balanced your network of personal relationships is. People differ markedly in what sort of network they feel comfortable with, but in general a reasonably wide pattern involving home, work and social activity, with different levels of intensity and closeness in each of those areas, is best at protecting you from loss, stress and the development of psychological disorders.

Stage 3: Testing out your analysis

Now you can continue examining your relationships in practice, as both participant and observer. Taking each relationship in turn, try to monitor what happens the next time you have contact. Use the questions above to explore how the contact went. Try to behave as naturally as possible and not to alter things. If it is difficult both to take part and to observe, then set aside some time afterwards to go through what happened. Pick a specific and time-limited period of contact to examine, rather than looking at the whole relationship.

Were your predictions about the relationship correct? If not, what aspects were different and what surprised you?

Remember that at this stage you are not trying to change things, just to get as detailed and accurate a picture as you can of how your relationships actually work.

It may take you some time to gather the evidence you need. Some relationships, though important, may involve quite infrequent contact.

Stage 4: Deciding what to change and when

Once you have got a complete picture, take some time to consider which relationships you would like to change, which are the most important ones to change and which you think you have the most chance of altering. At this stage, be quite optimistic; don't assume that certain relationships will be impossible to shift.

For each, consider what part you play in maintaining the current relationship and how much you are prepared to change.

At this point, you may ask: why bother changing? There are two very important reasons.

- First, having a rich, balanced, safe and supportive network of relationships is one of the most important ways of maintaining your well-being and your psychological health. Research from many different areas and in many different disorders shows that having a good social network and supportive but balanced interpersonal relationships is an excellent protective against adversity.

- Second, one of the themes that runs through this book is that Anorexia Nervosa is centrally linked with *beliefs and feelings about control*. If you feel in control of your life, your future, your relationships, it will be easier to give up your Anorexia Nervosa. If you feel out of control, overwhelmed, intruded upon, then Anorexia Nervosa can seem your best option. Trying to make some shifts in your relationships may help this sense of control. It is important to emphasise that this is not about being controlling in your relationships; you have to play your part in being open and balanced.

Stage 5: Starting to make changes

There are two main ways of doing this.

- You can begin to make small changes and monitor what happens. For example, if you have decided you would like more contact with your grandmother, start to make more regular phone calls and monitor how things go. Even if it is a relationship that you have previously given up on, if you would like it to be rekindled, then have another go. If it's a relationship with a friend where your assessment has been that you give a great deal and receive very little back, try setting some limits. Start occasionally saying 'no'. Again, monitor what happens.
- The second way is to put all your cards on the table. Gather all the information you have learned about

one relationship and try to discuss this with the individual involved. Be open and not too challenging about this. Use statements such as 'This is the way I see things', and ask questions such as 'Have I got it right?' 'Is your view different?' Obviously, this is easier to do when you increase rather than decrease intensity and frequency of contact, and it is also more appropriate when the relationship is one in your close interpersonal circle, e.g. a partner, parent etc.

CHAPTER SUMMARY

- Interpersonal relationships are an extremely important aspect of human life, and a full, balanced network of relationships is a very good way of protecting your well-being.

- Whether or not your close relationships have anything to do with the development of your eating disorder, they will almost inevitably be markedly affected by the fact that you have Anorexia Nervosa.

- Improving your personal relationships will help your self-confidence and sense of control, and thereby help to make it easier for you to recover from Anorexia Nervosa.

HOMEWORK ASSIGNMENT FOR STEP 9

- Continue to keep your food diary and work towards the 'principles of normal eating'.
- Work through the five-stage plan outlined in this step. You may find it helpful to refer back to Step 7 on 'Developing assertiveness' in working out how to approach and talk to the individuals in your circle.
- If you find it very stressful to approach individuals openly, as described in the second option in Stage 5, try the anxiety-management techniques outlined in Step 8; or try using the first option until you feel confident enough to tackle direct discussion.
- Draw your interpersonal maps and practise different versions of these.

REFLECTIONS FROM STEP 9

- What have I learned?

_____

_____

_____

_____

_____

_____

- How can I put what I have learned into practice?

_____

_____

_____

_____

_____

_____

- What can I do differently as a result of reading this chapter?

_____

_____

_____

_____

_____

_____

_____

Step 10

Coping strategies for the future

The fluctuating nature of Anorexia Nervosa means that you may experience relapses during self-help or professional treatment. One of the themes of cognitive behavioural therapy is that it is not a cure – for Anorexia Nervosa or any other disorder. Cognitive behavioural therapy (CBT) is a set of skills and principles to learn and apply in therapy that can have a long-lasting and positive impact, following the completion of active therapy, to support your continued and sustained recovery. CBT can be applied to everyday life, and the benefit of putting these skills into practice in day-to-day life does not end once formal therapy or self-help is completed; it includes strategies for coping with setbacks. It is not defeatist to experience relapses, only realistic, and you are more likely to overcome these difficulties if you have prepared ways of coping with them in advance.

Preparing for crisis moments

Donna, a thirty-five-year-old housewife, suffered from Anorexia Nervosa for approximately four years before seeking help. She had been shown the 'principles of healthy eating', but although in theory she understood them, she found it very difficult to put them into practice. She had been able to sit down and write rational alternatives to her negative automatic thoughts; however, when faced with the reality of challenges in daily life, she often reverted to familiar past ways of thinking.

Look back at the anxiety curve, which relates to the increasing urge to restrict (Figures 8.4 and 8.5). Imagine yourself in a situation where you have a very strong urge not to eat what everyone else is eating – or anything at all. You may feel you need to stay in control, and that if you eat normally you might overeat and feel fat and terrible. You may have attempted to rationalise negative thoughts, but still the drive to restrict is overpowering.

At this point, you need to be able quickly to stop your train of thought and realise that you do actually have a choice in your decision to restrict or not; and then to distract yourself from the preoccupation with eating/not eating. Step 3 on negative automatic thoughts will hopefully have helped you to be more aware of the ways in which you think, and thus make it easier to break the cycle of unhelpful thought patterns. Here we introduce the next step in the coping strategy, which will direct you away from focusing on the drive to restrict your intake.

1. This exercise requires a few small cards (postcards cut in half would work) or you could use the notes facility on your mobile phone/tablet/PC.

2. Write on each one a distracting activity that you can do at any time, without preparation.

3. The purpose of this exercise activity is to sort the distraction activities into one of the three categories listed below. Try to think of at least three activities for each category.

4. Some people find it useful to have different sets of cards – one set for home, and another for work etc. – as some activities (e.g. going to bed!) are not appropriate in all situations. Some examples are given here to help you.

Category 1: Things I know are helpful, e.g.
- Doing your relaxation podcast
- Listening to music
- Going to bed

Category 2: Things that I enjoy doing, e.g.
- Taking a bath
- Drawing
- Reading a chapter of a novel

Category 3: Things on my 'to do' list, e.g.
- Writing a letter
- Housework (be specific, e.g. vacuuming)
- Phoning a friend
- Writing a diary

Put the cards into a box or your bag, where you can easily get to them as you need them. Another suggestion is to take a photo on your mobile phone so that you have access to the cards at all times (if you have them recorded in a notes section on your phone, you can access that quite easily).

The strategy described above helps you to discover that you do have a choice and there are alternatives available to cope with tension and stress.

Long-term coping: a maintenance plan

You may by this time be feeling that you 'should' be improving but have perhaps not been able to make great changes in your thoughts and behaviour. It is normal to feel some distress at the prospect of being free from Anorexia Nervosa – we have seen repeatedly during this manual (from the personal experiences of many individuals) how it gives people a sense of control that may be otherwise lacking in their lives, and how it often comes to dominate life. It can seem difficult to imagine replacing the perceived advantages on your eating disorder with alternative ways of coping. Change can be frightening and involves uncertainty and risk, which is uncomfortable, and it's natural to feel hesitant at times. You are certainly not failing if you are experiencing difficulties in putting these principles into practice. Do not give up: persevere, practise and recognise the progress you are making, and work to build upon this step by step.

By now you will have developed a better understanding of your Anorexia Nervosa, and be able to recognise that eating problems may recur at times of stress. It may be helpful to regard your eating problems as an 'Achilles' heel' – a vulnerable area; your coping mechanism in times of difficulty. This does not mean you can never get better; it just means that you might have to be more aware of your reaction to stressful situations.

You will hopefully have discovered while working through this manual that certain strategies can help you regain control over eating. The strategies covered are an important resource to reflect upon, establish and apply continuously – especially in the two circumstances detailed below:

1. if you sense you are at risk of relapse, or
2. if your eating problem has deteriorated.

At such times there will often be some unsolved difficulty underlying your relapse or fear of relapse. A helpful response would therefore be twofold:

1. First, examine what is happening in your life and look for any events or difficulties that might be of relevance. Once these have been identified, consider all possible solutions to these problems and construct an appropriate plan of action.
2. In addition, you could use one or more of the following strategies to help you challenge current eating disorder thoughts and behaviours and help to regain control over your recovery. Some of these will sound familiar to you, as they echo guidance given in Step 2

of this manual. You may well find it helpful to go right back to these basic points when you find yourself in difficulty.

Set some time aside to re-evaluate your progress every day or so. Some strategies may have worked; some may not. If you find that something isn't working, don't berate yourself for failure; try something else.

Additional coping strategies

1. Recommence your intake, using the food diary format set out in Step 2 when you eat it.
2. Try to eat in company, not alone.
3. Stick to eating three or four planned meals each day, plus one or two planned snacks. Try to have these meals and snacks at predetermined times, in the sequence: breakfast, mid-morning snack, lunch, mid-afternoon snack, dinner, supper.
4. Plan your days ahead. Avoid both long periods of unstructured time and overbooking. If you are feeling at risk of losing control, plan your meals in advance so that you know exactly what and when you will be eating. In general, you should try to keep one step ahead of the problem.
5. Try to eat at least four starch-based meals/snacks per day, and if possible five or six. Starch is better than high-sugar foods at normalising hunger/satiety.
6. Try not to eat all or most of your calories at one

time. There is a tendency for calories taken over a short period of time, with long periods of fasting in between, to lead to periods of low blood pressure, lethargy and low mood.

7. Introduce different or new foods into your diet regularly. Try to remember that food can be enjoyed for different tastes and textures, and isn't just for fuel and weight gain. If this is not possible while weight is being gained, leave this stage until weight gain has been established; but do be sure to include it!

8. Try not to do anything else while you eat, except socialising – remember that meals are times of important social contact. For instance, try not to watch television, read books, computers or magazines. It is usually all right to listen to music but you should try to concentrate on enjoying the meal. In time, you can build upon this and use mindfulness techniques to work towards recognising flavours and enjoying the meal, knowing you are providing self-care and fuelling your body's basic needs.

9. Try to refrain from weighing yourself more than once a week. Remember that fluctuations of up to 1 kg (2.2 lb) either up or down are quite normal; therefore, if you weigh yourself too often you may feel that you are gaining or losing weight when you are merely monitoring this daily variability. Remember that short periods of severe dieting tend to lead to transient weight loss of fluid, and, similarly, resuming normal eating will lead to temporary rapid weight gain.

10. Remember that each time you restrict and lose weight you tend to lose equal amounts of fat and muscle from your body. When you start to regain weight, initially it is nearly all fat that you put back on. This means that each time you diet, lose weight and then regain weight, the percentage of your body that is composed of fat increases.

11. If you are over-thinking about your shape, ask yourself whether this is because you are anxious or depressed. You probably tend to feel fat when things are not going well. See whether you can identify any current problems and do something positive to solve or at least minimise them.

12. Try not to be 'phobic' about your body. Do not avoid looking in mirrors or using communal changing rooms.

13. If possible, confide in someone. Explain your present predicament. A trouble shared is a trouble halved. You would not mind any friend of yours sharing his or her problems with you, would you?

Take some time just now to highlight which of these strategies are most helpful to you. When you find yourself in difficulties, or going through a relapse, try to use them before seeking professional help; remember, you have used them with benefit in the past. But if you do need further help with your eating problem, do contact your GP or local self-help group. Contact details for some organisations that could put you in touch with a local group are given at the end of this book.

Ways to relax

Learning to switch off, particularly from our own thought processes, is not as easy as it sounds. It is particularly difficult for someone with Anorexia Nervosa, as these inner thoughts are very insistent and constant. However, there are many techniques for relaxation, such as aromatherapy, and one of them is going to suit you. Remember that worrying about not being able to relax will jeopardise your chances of any technique being effective.

Before you attempt any of these relaxation techniques, be aware of why you must give time to yourself. Many people with Anorexia Nervosa make unreasonable demands of themselves and have little patience with what they perceive as their weaknesses. Learning how to be kind to yourself can be helpful, so it is important for you to prioritise your relaxation periods within your daily routine. If you struggle to give yourself time to switch off, you may become very distressed and tired, and feel your motivation to change begin to diminish. Try to regard these periods as a form of battery recharging, and as essential to your progress as drinking enough water.

Aromatherapy

Aromatherapy has become incredibly popular over recent years, and aromatherapy products are now widely available. The basic principle of aromatherapy is that the fragrances of essential oils can be used to improve health, and it has been shown to be particularly effective when dealing with stress and anxiety. Camomile and lavender oils are particularly good for treating anxiety and aiding relaxation, and blend well together. However, when using pure essential oils, it is important to avoid the undiluted oils making contact with the skin; and they should *never* be taken internally.

A good way to use them is to run a warm bath and add five drops of each to the running water. Alternatively, you could buy ready-made bath oils and bubble baths, which are available from most department stores and pharmacies, and are ready formulated to treat particular conditions.

Another excellent method is to invest in an aromatherapy oil burner, which allows the scent vapours to permeate the room. If you choose this method, you will need to invest in a carrier oil, such as wheat germ, to dilute the main oil, or in a water-based incense burner. Add two teaspoons of carrier oil to three drops of camomile and two of juniper, which has a very clean, peaceful scent.

Oils and oil burners are available from most health shops, as are books that give further details of the properties of essential oils and how to use them. If you feel that aroma-therapy is right for you, you would be well advised to consult a trained aromatherapist, who can describe the oils that suit you and your needs. An aromatherapist will also take into consideration your lifestyle and circumstances, and the fact that you are seeking to combat Anorexia Nervosa, when prescribing treatment.

Meditation and mindfulness

When you are meditating or practising mindfulness, you are intensely aware of yourself and your surroundings. Mindfulness is the ability to be fully present and aware of where we are and what we're doing. We try not to react to what is going on around us when we are being mindful and in the present moment. If you can practise on a daily basis, you may find that it becomes easier. Whenever you are aware of what you are experiencing you are being mindful. Meditation and mindfulness often appeals to the person with Anorexia Nervosa, in that it teaches you to focus within yourself, rather than on your physical body. As you become expert in meditation, you will be able to stop the flow of negative and self-defeating thoughts that dominate your consciousness, and this can provide a tremendous feeling of release. It will also enable you to examine the way that you think in a more dispassionate way, rather than being at the mercy of it.

Being taught is the ideal way to learn this art, though it is important to find a teacher who is trained and whom you trust. Self-help guides are also available. Meditation requires 100 per cent concentration and may be based on a visual image or a repetition of sounds or words, known as a mantra. This need have no significance other than that the sound appeals to you and induces a sense of peacefulness. Many who have learned to meditate report increased feelings of self-confidence as well as reduced anxiety and susceptibility to stress. Furthermore, as you are undergoing a period of great change in your life, regular practice of meditation will help you to feel more in control of your situation and more 'grounded'.

Another useful feature of meditation is that, once you have mastered it, you will be able to devise 'quick fixes' for yourself. For example, if you know that your anxiety levels will rise prior to a meal, even to the extent that it just seems easier to avoid the whole thing altogether, you could devise a five-minute meditation, perhaps based on an image or a mantra, that will release the anxiety and allow you to face the task ahead.

Relaxation apps

There are many excellent relaxation apps available, with soundtracks varying from whale song to spoken journeys. If you find it hard to relax and to concentrate on abstract sound, a spoken relaxation recording will probably suit you. Below is an example of a relaxation script, which you can adapt to suit your needs or use as a springboard for creating your own. Remember to choose images and sensations that appeal to you, and that you associate with being relaxed.

> *Close your eyes and imagine yourself standing on a newly mown lawn on a warm summer's morning. You can feel the springy grass, still slightly wet from the dew, beneath your feet. You can feel the sun, already warm, across the back of your shoulders. Take a deep breath and suck in the smell of the grass and the sunlight on your skin. Through your closed eyelids the sunlight seems red.*

As you breathe out you become aware of the sounds of birds singing in the trees, and in the far distance you can hear the hum of a lawnmower. Otherwise there is silence all around. Look around you and see that you are standing on a lawn before a magnificent country house. Look at the way the sun lights up the stonework, and at the clear blue sky above it. In the distance you can see the road leading from the house through lush green parkland. In the far, far distance is the sea, glittering at the horizon. Your body feels very light and clean, and you move easily, almost without effort.

Take another deep breath and begin to walk away from the house. Feel the grass under your feet give way to sun-warmed stone and see that you are standing at the top of a shallow flight of stone steps. These steps lead down to an ornamental garden. As you slowly descend them, you begin to hear the splashing of a fountain. The sound is very cool and light, and makes you feel refreshed.

As you reach the bottom step, you breathe in the fragrance of summer flowers. All around you is vibrant colour — bright yellows and violets and pinks and reds. Stems reach up from stone urns and from flowerbeds. You walk along the stone-flagged paths that surround these flowerbeds. Trail your fingers across the heads of the flowers and feel the softness of the petals. Breathe deeply. Take slow steps and allow yourself to sink into the atmosphere. Stay as long as you like.

When you are ready to move on, take the right-hand path from the garden and let it lead you through the trees. Under their canopy it is very cool, and the noise of the water becomes louder. As you emerge into the sunlight, you are standing in front of a stone fountain, set in the middle of an ornamental lake. The water rises high, and you can feel flecks of spray on your arms and face. Take a seat beside the lake and let the spray cool your shoulders as you turn your face to the sun. Take a deep breath and smile. This is your own, peaceful place, and you can stay as long as you wish.

When you are ready to go, return through the trees to the garden. Feel the cool stones under your feet and smell the flowers as you pass. Climb slowly back up to the lawn. Take your time. As you emerge from the top step you note that the sun is higher in the sky, and the grass is warmer and drier beneath your feet. As you walk closer to the house, you see that the hallway looks cool and dark and inviting. Walk slowly towards the house, feeling the sun on your face. Hear the birds in the trees and the distant lawnmower, almost imperceptible now. Look up and see the faraway glitter of the sea. As you walk, get ready to say goodbye to the garden. As your feet touch the smooth flagstones of the hall floor, slowly open your eyes.

At the end of the 'relaxation journey', always give yourself a couple of minutes to readjust to where you are.

If you prefer to construct your own journey, cast your mind back to a time and place where you were happy. Maybe you would prefer to imagine yourself on a beach, with the sand between your toes and the sound of the waves in your ears. Maybe you like mountains or rivers. Don't worry about creating perfectly detailed pictures in your mind's eye. The important thing is that you can, even to a small extent, sink into this imaginative landscape and recreate, in your imagination, sounds and scents. If the first time is a little disappointing, don't be discouraged. You will improve with practice. The important thing is to set aside some time, probably fifteen to twenty minutes, every day for this exercise.

Other suggestions

Gentle exercise is beneficial to relaxation, so long as it is undertaken for the purposes of winding down, rather than burning off calories. Reading can also be effective if it is done purely for enjoyment. Alternatively, you might want to consider taking up a new hobby. Try to find something that does not require vast amounts of preparation or money. Ideally, you want something that you can pick up at any point during the day. Resist the notion that it must be educational or improving in some way; this is something just for you. Even completing jigsaw puzzles might do the trick, if it is absorbing enough to distract you from worries and negative thought patterns.

Recognising negative behaviours

There is no easy solution to the problem of reverting to old ways of thinking and old routines. We noted at the very beginning of this step that it would be unrealistic to expect there will not be challenges and ups and downs along the way. Sometimes you may feel that you have achieved nothing and are as trapped by your Anorexia Nervosa as you were when you started trying to change. Try not to let these feelings overwhelm you, and keep to the forefront of your mind that what you are trying to achieve is not easy. The following summary points may help you to get back on track and persevere with your efforts.

Accept rocky progress

You may have very high expectations of yourself and expect yourself to be able to achieve whatever you set your mind to. You can overcome your Anorexia Nervosa; but you may not be able to do it as quickly and smoothly as you would wish. If there are issues that you stumble over, such as that of breaking the habit of constantly weighing yourself, do not give up. Begin each stage of change, even if you are doing so for the umpteenth time, in the state of mind in which you first approached it. You will have breakthroughs, and you will make progress. The hard part is accepting that sometimes this progress will be slow, and sometimes it will seem to be non-existent. Remember that even picking up this book is itself a sign that you are moving forward. It has taken strength and courage to get this far, so try to keep that in mind, if you can.

Reverting back to old ways of thinking

Sometimes you may find yourself becoming reabsorbed into your old ways of thinking. If this happens, look back over your diary and, if necessary, work through Steps 3 and 4 again on 'Challenging the way you think'. It is hard to change the way you see things, but it is far from impossible. However, be wary of the tendency to revert out of the fear of change. You will be happier, and more in control of your life, without your Anorexia Nervosa; so resist any notion that Anorexia Nervosa is something that offers you refuge and safety.

Depression

Constant or increasing depression will hinder your attempts to change, as it will rob you of motivation and make you feel that your efforts are hopeless. If you find this to be the case, consult your GP, who will be able to offer advice on how to treat your depression. Don't fall into the trap of thinking that you will work on your Anorexia Nervosa once your depression has lifted. Remember that there will never be a time that seems 'right' for making these difficult changes, and once you have made the commitment to change, don't let anything stand in your way.

Changes in circumstance or lifestyle

Many people feel very stressed by change, whether it takes the form of a new job, a new member of the family, or a move of house. In such situations, we often reach out for the familiar, clinging to old routines and behaviours, and in most cases this is a harmless part of the readjustment process. However, for the person with Anorexia Nervosa, it is not harmless, and could be the beginning of your sliding back into the grip of the illness. Be kind to yourself, and aware that lifestyle changes are stressful for everyone. Keep going with your efforts; remember that being free from Anorexia Nervosa will leave you much better equipped to cope with life events, including further changes of circumstance, in the future.

Reflections from Step 10

- What have I learned?

_____

_____

_____

_____

_____

_____

_____

- How can I put what I have learned into practice?

_____

_____

_____

_____

_____

_____

- What can I do differently as a result of reading this chapter?

_____

_____

_____

_____

_____

_____

A Final Word

The model for treatment contained in this book has been proven to help many individuals to recover from eating disorders, and we hope that by the time you are reading this, it is a positive support in your journey to recovery. However, if this is not your experience, please know this does not mean that you cannot get better or that your eating disorder is untreatable. The fact that you have persisted thus far and engaged in this self-help treatment shows great progress and the strength you possess to overcome the eating disorder.

If you feel that you are back at square one, or have made a small step in the right direction but find yourself unable to move any further, now is the time to seek professional help.

Your first step may be your GP or family doctor. If you feel that your doctor is unable to help you, ask to be referred to a specialist, or contact an organisation such as Beat, the UK's eating disorder charity (www.beateatingdisorders.org. uk). They will be able to offer advice and put you in touch with groups and specialists in your area.

It is very important that you do not become discouraged. Try to take each day as it comes, and count your successes, not your failures. Enlist support from friends and family, and maintain awareness of your situation, your state of mind and your physical health. And remember that many, many thousands of men and women have been in just such circumstances as yours and have recovered and gone on to lead fulfilling and happy lives. You can do that too.

Useful books

Gillian Butler, *Overcoming Social Anxiety and Shyness: A Self-help Guide Using Cognitive Behavioural Techniques*, 2nd edition, Robinson, 2016.

Peter Cooper, *Overcoming Bulimia Nervosa and Binge Eating: A Self-help Guide Using Cognitive Behavioural Techniques*, 3rd edition, Robinson, 2014.

Melanie Fennell, *Overcoming Low Self-Esteem: A Self-help Guide Using Cognitive Behavioural Techniques*, 2nd edition, Robinson, 2016.

Paul Gilbert, *Overcoming Depression: A Self-help Guide Using Cognitive Behavioural Techniques*, 3rd edition, Robinson, 2009.

Helen Kennerley, *Overcoming Anxiety: A Self-help Guide Using Cognitive Behavioural Techniques*, 2nd edition, Robinson, 2014.

Derrick Silove and Vijaya Manicavagasar, *Overcoming Panic: A Self-help Guide Using Cognitive Behavioural Techniques*, 2nd edition, Robinson, 2017.

Gillian Todd, *An Introduction to Coping with Eating Problems: A Self-help Guide Using Cognitive Behavioural Techniques*, 2nd edition, Robinson, 2017.

Useful contact details

Eating Disorders Association (BEAT)
www.beateatingdisorders.org.uk
Tel: 0808 801 0677

Scottish Association for Mental Health (SAMH)
www.samh.org.uk
Tel: 0141 530 1000

Priory Group (specialists in eating disorder treatment)
www.priorygroup.com
Tel: 0800 787 0186

Extra monitoring sheets

Diary 1: Monitoring Your Eating

	Portion	Vomit	Laxative	Exercise
Breakfast:				
Snack:				
Lunch:				

Evening meal:			
Snack:			
Totals:			

Diary 1: Monitoring Your Eating

	Portion	Vomit	Laxative	Exercise
Breakfast:				
Snack:				
Lunch:				

	Evening meal:	Snack:	Totals:

Diary 1: Monitoring Your Eating

	Portion	Vomit	Laxative	Exercise
Breakfast:				
Snack:				
Lunch:				

Evening meal:		Snack:	Totals:

Diary 1: Monitoring Your Eating

	Portion	Vomit	Laxative	Exercise
Breakfast:				
Snack:				
Lunch:				

	Evening meal:	Snack:	Totals:

Diary 1: Monitoring Your Eating

	Portion	Vomit	Laxative	Exercise
Breakfast:				
Snack:				
Lunch:				

Evening meal:			
Snack:			
Totals:			

Diary 1: Monitoring Your Eating

		Portion	Vomit	Laxative	Exercise
Breakfast:					
Snack:					
Lunch:					

	Evening meal:	Snack:	Totals:

Diary 1: Monitoring Your Eating

	Portion	Vomit	Laxative	Exercise
Breakfast:				
Snack:				
Lunch:				

Evening meal:		Snack:	Totals:

Diary 2: Challenging automatic thoughts

Date	Emotions	Situation	Automatic Thoughts

Diary 2: Challenging automatic thoughts

Date	Emotions	Situation	Automatic Thoughts

Diary 2: Challenging automatic thoughts

Date	Emotions	Situation	Automatic Thoughts

Diary 2: Challenging automatic thoughts

Date	Emotions	Situation	Automatic Thoughts

Diary 2: Challenging automatic thoughts

Date	Emotions	Situation	Automatic Thoughts

Diary 2: Challenging automatic thoughts

Date	Emotions	Situation	Automatic Thoughts

Index